WILLIAMS-SONOMA

HORS D'OEUVRE

RECIPES AND TEXT
BRIGIT L. BINNS

GENERAL EDITOR
CHUCK WILLIAMS

PHOTOGRAPHS
NOEL BARNHURST

SIMON & SCHUSTER • **SOURCE**

NEW YORK • LONDON • TORONTO • SYDNEY • SINGAPORE

CONTENTS

CANAPÉS

DIPS AND SPREADS

WRAPS AND SKEWERS

INTRODUCTION

A good hors d'oeuvre has just a few requirements: It should be small, appealing, and delicious to eat. The French have another, more charming term for finger food beside hors d'oeuvre: *amuse-bouche,* or "amuse-the-mouth." All the recipes in this cookbook aim to do just that. You'll find classic recipes such as miniature quiches, new potatoes with caviar, shrimp cocktail. Some recipes are simple and rustic, just a radish topped with herb-flavored butter; some are casual and flavorful, a dollop of gingery eggplant dip on a carrot stick; and the chapters of elegant hors d'oeuvres and of stylish wraps and skewers will inspire you when you're planning even the most elaborate affair.

Each recipe in this book is kitchen-tested and highlights a particular ingredient, term, or technique. A chapter of basics in the back of the book offers detailed guidance for hosting a formal party, complete with a selection of cocktails and other drinks. Try any of these recipes and your guests will return for more.

Chuck Williams

THE CLASSICS

The definition of a classic? Something that stands the test of time. In this chapter you'll find some of the most enduring pleasures of simpler days, delectable hors d'oeuvres that instantly come to mind and unfailingly whet the appetite. What better way to accompany a tall flute of Champagne or a dry martini?

NEW POTATOES WITH CAVIAR
AND CRÈME FRAÎCHE

Pour water to a depth of 3 inches (7.5 cm) into a saucepan and bring to a boil. Add 1 tablespoon salt. Put the potatoes into a steamer basket and set the basket over the boiling water. Cover and steam until the potatoes are tender when pierced with the tip of a knife, 15–18 minutes. Do not overcook. Remove the basket from the pan and let the potatoes cool to room temperature.

Cut a very thin slice off one end of each potato to make a flat base on which it will stand upright. Cut a slightly thicker slice off the opposite end or halve the potato if it is on the large side. Using a small spoon or the small end of a melon baller, slightly hollow out the circle or oval of flesh.

Arrange the potatoes, hollow sides up, on a platter. Spoon about ½ teaspoon crème fraîche into each hollow and smooth it slightly. Top each with ¼ teaspoon caviar, and slide the ends of 2 chive lengths into the crème fraîche. Serve at once.

MAKES 20–40 ROOM-TEMPERATURE BITES

Coarse sea salt

20 small red or white new potatoes, each about 1 inch (2.5 cm) in diameter, unpeeled

3½ tablespoons crème fraîche

2 tablespoons beluga, osetra, or sevruga caviar or other fish roe such as North American whitefish or tobiko (about 1 oz/30 g)

40 lengths fresh chives, each ½ inch (12 mm) long

NEW POTATOES
Potatoes dug in spring and early summer that go directly from field to market are known as new potatoes. They are firm and moist, with thin skins and a fresh flavor. New potatoes range in size from smaller than a golf ball to five times that size and are ideal for steaming or boiling. Not all tiny potatoes are new, but any potato 1–1½ inches (2.5–4 cm) in diameter will also work well in this dish.

THREE-CHEESE FILO TRIANGLES

1 cup (8 oz/250 g) whole-milk ricotta cheese

6 oz (185 g) feta cheese, crumbled

6 oz (185 g) smoked mozzarella cheese, cut into ¼-inch (6-mm) cubes

2 shallots, minced

⅓ cup (½ oz/15 g) coarsely chopped fresh flat-leaf (Italian) parsley

1 egg, lightly beaten

Salt and freshly ground pepper

7 sheets frozen filo dough, thawed *(far right)*

⅓ cup (3 oz/90 g) unsalted butter, melted

In a large bowl, combine the ricotta, feta, mozzarella, shallots, parsley, egg, a generous ¼ teaspoon salt, and ¼ teaspoon pepper. Using 2 forks or your hands, toss thoroughly until all the filling ingredients are uniformly combined.

Preheat the oven to 350°F (180°C). Lightly oil 1 or 2 baking sheets. Cut the whole stack of thawed filo lengthwise into quarters. Each strip will be about 3½ inches (9 cm) wide. Working with 1 filo strip at a time and keeping the others covered with a barely damp towel, place the filo strip on a dry work surface. Brush it lightly but thoroughly with the melted butter.

Place about 1 tablespoon of the filling 1 inch (2.5 cm) from the bottom edge. Fold the lower right corner of the pastry up and over the filling, forming a triangle. Roll the triangle straight forward, then again on a diagonal. Continue folding, forming a triangle each time, until you reach the end of the strip. Transfer to a prepared baking sheet and brush the top of the triangle with a little more butter. Use the remaining filo and filling to make the remaining triangles, placing them on the baking sheet(s).

Bake the triangles until golden brown, about 20 minutes. Let cool for 10 minutes (the filling will be very hot), then serve.

Make-Ahead Tip: The unbaked triangles can be frozen for up to 1 week in airtight containers, separated by layers of parchment (baking) or waxed paper. When you are ready to serve them, bake them straight from the freezer, adding 5 minutes or so to the baking time.

MAKES 28 WARM BITES

WORKING WITH FILO

Filo is a paper-thin pastry of Greek origin, similar to other pastries used throughout the eastern Mediterranean. It is available in the freezer section of many well-stocked food stores and in Greek and Middle Eastern markets. Most 1-pound (500-g) boxes contain about 20 sheets, each one measuring 14 by 18 inches (35 by 45 cm). For best results, let the pastry thaw very slowly, in the refrigerator if time allows. When working with filo, be sure to keep the unused sheets covered with a barely damp kitchen towel to prevent them from drying out and becoming brittle.

LEEK AND RED PEPPER MINI QUICHES

Place the Cheddar pastry on a lightly floured work surface and shape into a smooth ball. Divide in half. Roll out half into a large round ⅛ inch (3 mm) thick, pushing the dough outward from the center and rotating it about a quarter turn each time you roll, sprinkling more flour underneath as needed. Using a 2-inch (5-cm) cookie cutter, cut out as many pastry rounds as possible and ease them very gently into the cups of a mini muffin pan. The bottoms should remain rounded and the dough edges flush with the rims. Gather up the scraps, reroll, cut out additional rounds, and line additional cups. Repeat with the remaining dough half, working in batches if necessary. You should have 48 lined cups in all.

Preheat the oven to 400°F (200°C). In a small sauté pan over medium-low heat, melt the butter. Add the leek and sauté gently, stirring occasionally, until it is tender but not browned, about 5 minutes. In a bowl, combine the leek, bell pepper, and cheese. In another bowl or large measuring cup, whisk the eggs until they are blended, then whisk in the cream, mustard, ¾ teaspoon salt, and cayenne. Add the egg mixture to the cheese mixture and whisk to combine. Pour 1 tablespoon of the filling into each of the pastry shells, evenly distributing the solids and liquid.

Bake the quiches until they are puffy and golden brown, about 20 minutes. Transfer to a rack to cool for 5–10 minutes (they will sink a little as they cool). To loosen them from the muffin cups, run a thin-bladed knife around the sides, then carefully lift out of the cups. (At this point, you can allow them to cool for an hour or two, and then reheat them in a 350°F/180°C oven for 10 minutes. They will not be as crisp, however.) Arrange on a platter and serve.

MAKES 48 WARM BITES

CHEDDAR PASTRY

In a food processor, pulse ¼ lb (125 g) white Cheddar cheese chunks until crumbly. Add 1½ cups (7½ oz/235 g) all-purpose (plain) flour and ¼ teaspoon salt. Pulse until cheese is finely crumbled. Add ½ cup (4 oz/125 g) chilled unsalted butter cut into pieces and pulse until it resembles fluffy bread crumbs. Drizzle 1 lightly beaten egg over mixture and pulse twice. Scrape down bowl sides. Sprinkle 2 tablespoons cold water over the mixture and pulse until a rough mass forms. If the mixture doesn't come together, add another tablespoon of water.

Cheddar Pastry *(far left)*

1½ tablespoons butter

1 leek, white part only, or 2 large shallots, finely chopped

½ small red bell pepper (capsicum), seeded and cut into ¼-inch (6-mm) dice

¼ lb (125 g) dry-aged white Cheddar cheese, grated

2 eggs

1½ cups (12 fl oz/375 ml) heavy (double) cream

¾ teaspoon Dijon mustard

Salt

⅛ teaspoon cayenne pepper

MOROCCAN-STYLE MEATBALLS

2 tablespoons olive oil

1 red onion, very finely chopped

1 lb (500 g) ground (minced) lamb

3 large cloves garlic, crushed through a press

2 eggs, lightly beaten

1 cup (1 oz/30 g) loosely packed fresh flat-leaf (Italian) parsley leaves, finely chopped

1 cup (1 oz/30 g) loosely packed fresh mint leaves, finely chopped, plus sprigs for garnish

2 tablespoons fine dried bread crumbs (page 111)

1½ teaspoons ground cumin

1 teaspoon ground cinnamon

Salt and freshly ground pepper (see Note)

Lemon wedges for squeezing and garnish

About 42 cocktail picks (optional)

In a frying pan over medium-low heat, warm the olive oil. Add the onion and sauté, stirring occasionally, until very soft, about 10 minutes. Transfer to a large bowl and let cool.

Add the lamb, garlic, eggs, parsley, chopped mint, bread crumbs, cumin, cinnamon, 1 teaspoon salt, and ½ teaspoon pepper to the onion. Combine the ingredients thoroughly with your hands (the only way to achieve an even distribution of the ingredients). Fry a small pinch of the mixture, taste, and adjust the seasoning with salt and pepper. Form the mixture into balls about the size of a walnut, rolling them very lightly in the palms of your hands. Place on a lightly oiled baking sheet with a shallow rim.

Preheat the broiler (grill). Place the meatballs about 4 inches (10 cm) from the heat source and broil (grill), turning once with tongs, until brown and crispy on both sides, about 10 minutes total. Remove the baking sheet from the broiler and transfer the meatballs to a platter.

Squeeze some lemon juice over the meatballs and arrange the remaining lemon wedges and mint sprigs on the platter. Using cocktail picks, skewer each meatball if desired. Serve at once.

Note: If doubling this recipe, use only 1½ times the amount of salt, not double the amount.

Make-Ahead Tip: The meatballs can be refrigerated for up to 4 hours before cooking. Remove from the refrigerator 15 minutes before cooking. If desired, cook and cool the meatballs, refrigerate them for up to 4 hours, and then reheat in a 350°F (180°C) oven until heated through, 10–20 minutes.

MAKES ABOUT 42 WARM BITES

PREPARING MEATBALLS

Although these meatballs are not a traditional dish of Morocco, the presence of mint, parsley, cinnamon, and cumin gives them a strong North African accent. Use a light hand when forming the balls, just as you would when shaping a hamburger patty. A gentle touch ensures that the meat is not compacted or overheated by contact with your hands, resulting in light and tender mouthfuls.

ENDIVE BOATS
WITH SMOKED SALMON

In a food processor, combine the salmon, cream cheese, crème fraîche, grated onion and juice, lemon juice, and ¼ teaspoon white pepper. Process to combine, stopping to scrape down the bowl sides as necessary. Taste and adjust the seasoning with salt and white pepper. (If the salmon is salty, you may not need to add any salt.) Pulse again to mix.

Arrange the endive leaves, wide ends facing inward, in concentric circles on a large round platter. Spoon the salmon mixture into a pastry (piping) bag fitted with a ¼-inch (6-mm) star tip (see page 21), and pipe a generous rosette of the salmon mousse onto the wide end of each leaf. Alternatively, spoon a tablespoon-sized dollop of the mousse onto the end of the leaf.

If desired, garnish with a few grains of salmon roe and a pinch of alfalfa sprouts pressed gently into the mousse. Serve at once.

Note: Grate onion on the finest holes of a box grater set over a plate to catch the juice. The result is almost like a purée. You will need about one-quarter of an onion to produce 2 teaspoons grated onion.

Make-Ahead Tip: If desired, the salmon mousse can be covered and refrigerated for up to 24 hours before topping the endive leaves. Leave the mousse at room temperature for 20 minutes before spooning it into the pastry bag.

MAKES 24 ROOM-TEMPERATURE BITES

½ lb (250 g) smoked salmon, slices and/or trimmings, coarsely chopped

½ cup (2¾ oz/80 g) whipped cream cheese

⅓ cup (3 oz/90 g) crème fraîche or sour cream

2 teaspoons finely grated yellow onion and juice (see Note)

2 tablespoons fresh lemon juice

Salt and freshly ground white pepper

24 large Belgian endive (chicory/witloof) leaves

1½ tablespoons salmon roe (optional)

Alfalfa sprouts for garnish (optional)

BELGIAN ENDIVE

Also known simply as endive, and called chicory in England, Belgian endive is a member of the large chicory family. It is grown by a labor-intensive method that requires forcing the roots to sprout in a cool, moist, darkened space in order to prevent the green chlorophyll from developing. The result is a harvest of pale, tightly furled, slightly conical shoots. Although most endives are creamy white with just a touch of yellowish green at the edges, a variety with pale burgundy tips is also available.

DEVILED EGGS WITH CAPERS

12 extra-large or jumbo eggs, as fresh as possible and preferably organic

3 tablespoons mayonnaise

1 teaspoon whole-grain mustard

1½ teaspoons Champagne vinegar

2 tablespoons capers, rinsed

1 tablespoon finely chopped fresh flat-leaf (Italian) parsley

1 anchovy fillet, soaked for 5 minutes in lukewarm water, drained, and patted dry (optional)

Fine sea salt

Scant ⅛ teaspoon cayenne pepper, or to taste

Carefully place the eggs in a wide, deep saucepan and add water to cover. Place over medium heat and bring to a boil. As soon as the water begins to boil, remove the pan from the heat, cover, and let stand for 11 minutes. Transfer the eggs to a bowl of iced water and let stand for 6 minutes. Strike each egg against the side of the bowl to crack the shell slightly. If desired, peel immediately, or let stand in the water for up to 1 hour. (They will be easier to peel if, after cracking the shell, they are allowed to stand in the water.)

Peel the eggs and cut in half lengthwise. Scoop out the yolks into a food processor. Reserve the whites, cut sides down, in a single layer to prevent splitting.

Add the mayonnaise, mustard, vinegar, capers, parsley, anchovy (if using), ¼ teaspoon salt if using anchovy or ½ teaspoon if not, and cayenne to the food processor. Pulse to combine, stopping to scrape down the sides of the bowl as necessary. Taste and adjust the seasoning, then spoon the mixture into a pastry (piping) bag fitted with a small star tip *(right)*.

No more than 15 minutes before serving time, pipe the mixture attractively into the egg white halves. Arrange the stuffed eggs on a platter and serve at once.

Make-Ahead Tips: The halved egg whites can be refrigerated, loosely covered with a kitchen towel, for up to 2 hours before filling. The egg yolk mixture can be refrigerated for up to 2 hours before piping. Leave the egg yolk mixture at room temperature for 20 minutes before spooning it into the pastry bag.

MAKES 24 ROOM-TEMPERATURE BITES

PASTRY BAG BASICS
To fill a pastry bag, first fit the bag with the selected tip. Roll down the top of the bag about halfway. Stand the bag in a large measuring pitcher and scoop the filling into it. Gently force the filling down almost to the tip, unroll the top of the bag, and twist the top to form a comfortable handle. Using even pressure, squeeze the top with one hand and guide the tip with the other. If you don't have a pastry bag, spoon the filling into a heavy-duty zippered plastic bag and snip off one of the bottom corners.

SHRIMP COCKTAIL

To make the sauce, in a bowl, combine the ketchup, horseradish, Tabasco, gin (if using), celery salt, sea salt, lemon juice, and parsley. Mix well and adjust the seasoning with horseradish, Tabasco, salt, or lemon juice to suit your taste. Cover and chill until serving, or up to 6 hours.

Peel the shrimp, leaving the last segment with tail fin intact to serve as a handle, and reserve the shells. Devein the shrimp if desired *(left)* and set aside, refrigerating them if the kitchen is very warm. In a large saucepan, combine the reserved shrimp shells, water, 1 tablespoon of the kosher salt, the wine, peppercorns, coriander seeds, bay leaves, onion, tarragon, and lemon halves. Bring to a boil over high heat, reduce the heat to low, and simmer, uncovered, for 20 minutes to make a stock. Remove the pan from the heat and let stand for 30 minutes.

Strain the stock through a fine-mesh sieve into a clean saucepan. Place over high heat and bring to a boil. Add the shrimp and immediately remove from the heat. Cover the pan and "poach" the shrimp until they are pink and opaque, about 3 minutes. Fill a large bowl with ice water, and add the remaining 1 tablespoon kosher salt. With a skimmer or a slotted spoon, transfer the shrimp to the iced water and let cool for 3 minutes. Drain well and refrigerate on a tray lined with paper towels until ready to serve, or up to 1 hour. (If desired, freeze the shrimp stock in small quantities and use in recipes calling for fish stock.)

At serving time, transfer the sauce to a wide cup or ramekin and place on a platter. Hook the shrimp around the edge, tails toward the outside, and mound the remaining shrimp to the side of the sauce. Pass the platter, keeping cocktail napkins at the ready.

MAKES ABOUT 28 COLD BITES

DEVEINING SHRIMP

Deveining, or removing the dark, visible intestinal tract that runs along the outer curve of a shrimp, is primarily done for aesthetic reasons when the "vein" is black and clearly visible. To devein a peeled raw shrimp, simply run a small, sharp knife along the back, being careful not to cut too deeply into the flesh. Slip the tip of the knife under the vein, lift it, and then pull it free of the shrimp. Note that shrimp may also be deveined with the shell intact, by slitting the shell with a knife, or after cooking.

FOR THE SAUCE:

1 cup (10½ oz/330 g) ketchup

2½ teaspoons prepared horseradish, drained

½ teaspoon Tabasco sauce

1 teaspoon gin (optional)

½ teaspoon celery salt

¼ teaspoon sea salt

1 tablespoon fresh lemon juice

1 tablespoon chopped flat-leaf (Italian) parsley

1½ lb (750 g) large shrimp (prawns)

8 cups (64 fl oz/2 l) water

2 tablespoons kosher salt

1 cup (8 fl oz/250 ml) dry white wine or vermouth

1 tablespoon peppercorns

1 tablespoon coriander seeds

2 bay leaves

1 small yellow onion, sliced

4 fresh tarragon sprigs

1 lemon, halved

CRAB CAKES

3 tablespoons unsalted butter

2 celery stalks, finely chopped

2 tablespoons finely chopped yellow onion

1 tablespoon water, if needed

1 cup (8 fl oz/250 ml) heavy (double) cream

1½ tablespoons Dijon mustard

1½ tablespoons finely chopped jarred pimiento (sweet pepper)

Salt and freshly ground white pepper

1 egg, lightly beaten

1 lb (500 g) lump crabmeat *(far right)*

1¼ cups (5 oz/155 g) fine dried bread crumbs (page 111)

2 tablespoons vegetable oil

½ lemon

12–14 thin baguette slices (optional)

Saffron Aioli (page 40) for serving (optional)

In a small sauté pan over low heat, melt 1 tablespoon of the butter. Add the celery and onion, cover, and cook very gently until tender, about 10 minutes. Add the water if the vegetables begin to brown. Add the cream, raise the heat to medium, and simmer, stirring frequently to prevent the mixture from boiling over, until reduced and quite thick, about 5 minutes. Remove from the heat, pour into a heatproof bowl, and let cool.

Add the mustard, pimiento, ½ teaspoon salt, and ¼ teaspoon white pepper to the cooled cream mixture and mix well. Whisk in the egg, then add the crabmeat, breaking it up a little but leaving some lumps intact. Toss gently until evenly mixed.

Pour the bread crumbs onto a plate, spreading them in an even layer. Scoop up a golf ball–sized portion of the crab mixture and gently squeeze out any excess liquid. Shape into a small patty. The mixture will be quite wet and loose. Place the crab cake on the crumbs, then scoop more crumbs over the top. Using a spatula, carefully turn the cake over onto your palm, letting the excess crumbs fall back onto the plate. Turn the cake back over onto the spatula and slide it gently onto a platter. Repeat to make the remaining crab cakes, 12–14 in all. Cover and refrigerate for at least 1 hour, preferably 2 hours, or up to 3 hours.

In a large frying pan over medium-low heat, melt 1 tablespoon of the remaining butter with 1 tablespoon of the oil. When the foam subsides, gently slide half of the crab cakes into the pan. Cook the first sides until golden brown, 5–6 minutes. Turn and brown on the second sides, 4–5 minutes longer. Keep the first batch of cakes warm in a low oven. Wipe out the pan with a paper towel and repeat to make the second batch of crab cakes. Squeeze the lemon half over all the crab cakes and, if desired, serve each on a slice of baguette, perhaps topped with a small dollop of aioli.

MAKES 12–14 WARM BITES

CRABMEAT
Cooked fresh crabmeat may be purchased from a good fish purveyor. The best type for this recipe is lump crabmeat, which consists of large, snowy white pieces. Flake crabmeat, which is a mixture of white and somewhat darker meat in smaller pieces, is generally good but should be reserved for other uses. Before using crabmeat, check it carefully for cartilage and shell fragments and gently squeeze it to remove excess moisture.

SIMPLE BITES

An hors d'oeuvre can be as simple as a cherry tomato plucked off the vine on a summer evening or an assortment of olives picked up at a local delicatessen and lightly dressed. Here, intense and true flavors are more important than elaborate presentations, although almost anything that tastes wonderful looks good, too.

TOMATO AND BASIL BRUSCHETTA
28

RADISHES WITH CHERVIL BUTTER
31

OLIVES WITH ORANGE AND MARJORAM
32

MOZZARELLA WITH SUN-DRIED TOMATO
35

PROSCIUTTO-WRAPPED MELON BALLS
35

CROSTINI WITH TAPENADE
36

RADICCHIO AND MANCHEGO
QUESADILLAS
39

CHERRY TOMATO HALVES
WITH SAFFRON AIOLI
40

TOMATO AND BASIL BRUSCHETTA

Halve the tomatoes crosswise and gently squeeze out the seeds. Use a small spoon to scoop out any stubborn remaining seeds. Cut the tomato flesh into ¼-inch (6-mm) dice, discarding any tough, pale flesh near the core end. In a bowl, combine the tomatoes, garlic, ¾ teaspoon sea salt, ¼ teaspoon pepper, and olive oil. Toss to coat evenly, adding a little more olive oil if the mixture appears dry. Taste for seasoning and let stand at room temperature for at least 30 minutes or up to 1 hour, to allow the flavors to marry.

Preheat the oven to 350°F (180°C). Stack the basil leaves in a neat pile and roll the pile into a cigar shape. Thinly slice the "cigar" crosswise. Add the basil to the tomato mixture and toss to combine.

Arrange the baguette slices on a baking sheet and brush them lightly with olive oil. Bake until golden, 10–15 minutes. Let cool, then transfer to a serving platter and top each slice with 1 table-spoon of the tomato mixture. Serve at once.

Make-Ahead Tips: The tomato mixture can be made up to 1 hour ahead of serving time. The bread can be toasted the night before and kept in an airtight container at room temperature until serving time.

MAKES ABOUT 24 ROOM-TEMPERATURE BITES

8 small, ripe tomatoes, about 1½ lb (750 g), peeled if desired *(far left)* and cored

2 small or 1 large clove garlic, minced

Sea salt and freshly ground pepper

2 tablespoons extra-virgin olive oil

10 fresh basil leaves

24 thin baguette slices

Olive oil for brushing

PEELING TOMATOES
Whether or not to peel a tomato is largely a matter of taste. For raw tomato preparations such as this one, peeled tomatoes have a meatier texture, but unpeeled ones may have a fresher flavor. To peel tomatoes, bring a saucepan three-fourths full of water to a boil. Score a shallow X in the blossom end of each tomato, then blanch them in the boiling water just until the skins begin to wrinkle, 10–20 seconds. Scoop out the tomatoes, drain, let cool, and then peel.

RADISHES WITH CHERVIL BUTTER

FOR THE CHERVIL BUTTER:

¾ cup unsalted butter, at room temperature

½ teaspoon sea salt

3 tablespoons minced fresh chervil

16 radishes, chilled

Fresh chervil sprigs for garnish

To make the chervil butter, in a small bowl, stir together the butter, salt, and minced chervil until well mixed and creamy.

Remove a small sliver from the base and top of each radish, then halve it crosswise (across the "equator"). Each half will sit firmly and evenly with the larger cut side uppermost. Arrange the halved radishes on a platter, larger cut side up.

Spoon the chervil butter into a pastry (piping) bag fitted with a small star tip (see page 21). Pipe a small rosette of chervil butter in the center of each half.

Decorate the platter with chervil sprigs or, if desired, press a tiny frond of feathery chervil into the side of each chervil-butter rosette. Chill before serving.

Make-Ahead Tip: The butter-topped radishes may be refrigerated, uncovered, for up to 2 hours before serving.

Variation Tips: Substitute basil for the chervil, creating another wonderful flavoring for the butter. You may also serve the radishes with plain unsalted butter, a popular French snack.

MAKES 32 SMALL COLD BITES

RADISH VARIETIES

Some marvelous varieties of radish are now showing up in farmers' markets. A mix of colors and varieties would make an appealing plate— look for white, black, French Breakfast, and Misato Rose. Whichever variety you choose, look for firm radishes with smooth skin and unwilted green leaves. If you have a green thumb, take a look at the radish page of your favorite seed catalog.

OLIVES WITH ORANGE
AND MARJORAM

In a ceramic or glass bowl, combine the olives, orange zest and juice, orange oil, garlic (if using), ½ teaspoon salt, ¼ teaspoon pepper, marjoram, and olive oil. Toss well. Transfer to a serving bowl and serve.

Notes: Orange oil, painstakingly extracted from the zest of oranges, is sold in small quantities. A little goes a very long way. It is available from specialty-food shops and through mail-order catalogs. Any uneaten olives may be refrigerated in an airtight container for up to 4 days. Do not use ripe black pitted California olives for this recipe.

MAKES ABOUT 60 ROOM-TEMPERATURE BITES

1 lb (500 g) brine-cured green or black olives, drained

Grated zest and juice of 1 orange

⅛ teaspoon orange oil (see Notes)

2 cloves garlic, finely chopped (optional)

Salt and freshly ground pepper

1 tablespoon fresh marjoram leaves

2 tablespoons extra-virgin olive oil

OLIVES

Nowadays, many shoppers are blessed with a wide variety of cured olives at their markets. Among the most commonly available are the black Kalamata from Greece; the mild, green picholine and the tiny, black Niçoise from France; the Gaeta from Italy; and the Manzanillo from Spain. Two tasty olives that until relatively recently were not often seen outside their places of origin are the large, mild, green Bella di Cerignola from Italy and the herb-seasoned black olive typically labeled Moroccan.

MOZZARELLA WITH
SUN-DRIED TOMATO

20 tiny fresh mozzarella
balls *(bocconcini),* about
½ lb (250 g) total

20 oil-packed sun-dried
tomato halves, drained

40 cocktail picks

Halve the fresh mozzarella balls and cut each tomato lengthwise into 4 strips. Thread a strip of sun-dried tomato, half of a mozzarella ball, and another strip of sun-dried tomato onto each cocktail pick. Refrigerate the picks for up to 2 hours.

Serve the picks chilled or at cool room temperature.

MAKES 40 COLD OR ROOM-TEMPERATURE BITES

MOZZARELLA

Meaning "little mouthfuls" in Italian, *bocconcini* are the smallest form of creamy fresh mozzarella. The cheese is commonly packaged in water or whey, but can sometimes be found marinated in olive oil and herbs.

PROSCIUTTO-WRAPPED
MELON BALLS

1 large honeydew melon,
halved and seeded

8 slices prosciutto, about
¼ lb (125 g) total weight

48 cocktail picks (optional)

Using the large end of a melon baller, scoop the melon into balls, forming 48 balls in all. Cut each prosciutto slice lengthwise into thirds, and then crosswise in half to make 6 strips. You should have 48 strips in all. Chill the melon and prosciutto.

When ready to assemble the platter, wrap a strip of prosciutto around each melon ball. Use cocktail picks if desired to secure them together; they hold fairly well without them. Do not refrigerate after wrapping, or the juice from the melon will discolor the prosciutto and make it soggy.

MAKES 48 COLD BITES

PROSCIUTTO

This popular air-cured Italian ham is available in well-stocked delicatessens and Italian food stores. It is classically paired with melon and other fruits as an antipasto, or appetizer.

CROSTINI WITH TAPENADE

To make the tapenade, combine the olives, anchovies, capers, parsley, garlic, Cognac, lemon juice, and ½ teaspoon white pepper in a food processor. Pulse once or twice to combine roughly, then add the olive oil and pulse briefly, stopping to scrape down the bowl sides once or twice. The texture should be chunky, rather than a smooth purée. Set aside.

Preheat the oven to 350°F (180°C). Arrange the baguette slices on a baking sheet and coat them lightly with the olive oil spray, or brush lightly with olive oil. Bake until golden, 10–15 minutes.

Transfer the toasted baguette slices to a serving platter. Spread each one with about 1 tablespoon of the tapenade, then, if desired, crisscross 2 small strips of pimiento on top. Serve warm or at room temperature.

Make-Ahead Tip: The tapenade can be transferred to a nonaluminum bowl or a jar, tightly covered, and refrigerated for up to 48 hours. Return to room temperature for 15 minutes before serving.

MAKES 24 WARM OR ROOM-TEMPERATURE BITES

ANCHOVIES

These little fish, so important in Mediterranean cooking, are available preserved in two forms: packed in olive oil or in salt. Oil-packed anchovy fillets are widely available and need only to be rinsed in cool water and patted dry. Salt-packed anchovies, imported from Italy, must be filleted. To do this, hold each fish under running water and scrape off the fins and scales with a knife. Split the fish open lengthwise, separating it into two fillets, and lift out the backbone.

FOR THE TAPENADE:

1½ cups (7½ oz / 235 g) pitted mild brine-cured green olives such as Luques or picholines, black Niçoise olives, or a combination of several kinds

3 anchovy fillets, rinsed and patted dry

3 tablespoons capers, rinsed

1½ tablespoons coarsely chopped fresh flat-leaf (Italian) parsley

3 cloves garlic, finely chopped

1½ tablespoons Cognac or brandy

3 tablespoons fresh lemon juice

Freshly ground white pepper

¼ cup (2 fl oz / 60 ml) extra-virgin olive oil

24 thin baguette slices

Nonstick olive-oil or vegetable-oil cooking spray or olive oil

Pimiento (sweet pepper) strips for garnish (optional)

RADICCHIO AND MANCHEGO QUESADILLAS

2 tablespoons extra-virgin olive oil

1 tablespoon balsamic vinegar

½ clove garlic, minced

1 teaspoon minced fresh rosemary

Salt and freshly ground pepper

1 large head radicchio

2 tablespoons unsalted butter, melted

6 large flour tortillas

2½ tablespoons tapenade, homemade (page 36) or prepared, preferably made from green olives

¾ lb (375 g) Manchego cheese, coarsely grated (about 3 cups)

1 teaspoon fresh thyme leaves

Preheat the broiler (grill). In a small bowl, whisk together the oil, vinegar, garlic, rosemary, ⅛ teaspoon salt, and a pinch of pepper until blended.

Quarter the radicchio lengthwise into wedges; if it is very large, cut into 6 wedges. Each piece should be about 2 inches (5 cm) in diameter at its widest point. Swirl the wedges in a bowl of water and drain briefly in a colander.

Lightly brush all sides of each radicchio wedge with some of the oil mixture. Arrange on a broiler pan and place in the broiler about 4 inches (10 cm) from the heat source. Cook, watching closely, until slightly charred, 3½–5 minutes. Baste the tops of the wedges with more oil mixture, then turn them over and baste the other side. Continue to broil until deep brown and crisp on the surface but completely tender inside, 2–4 minutes longer.

Cut the radicchio crosswise into thin slivers. Assemble the melted butter, flour tortillas, tapenade, cheese, thyme, and pepper close at hand. Place a dry griddle over medium-high heat and brush with some of the butter. Thinly spread one side of a tortilla with one-third of the tapenade. Place on the griddle, tapenade side up. Scatter with one-third of the grated cheese, leaving a ¼-inch (6-mm) border around the tortilla's edge. Top with one-third each of the radicchio and the thyme and a generous grinding of pepper. Lay a tortilla on top and brush with more butter. Press down with a spatula and cook until the cheese begins to melt and the underside is mottled brown, 3–5 minutes. Flip and cook until the other side is golden, about 2 minutes longer. Transfer to a 200°F (95°C) oven to keep warm while you make the other 2 quesadillas. Cut each quesadilla into 6 equal wedges and serve at once.

MAKES 18 WARM BITES

MANCHEGO CHEESE

Manchego is made in the Spanish region of La Mancha from milk produced by the many sheep in the area. The cheese has a tangy, almost nutty flavor, firm texture, and lovely ivory to pale gold color. Its rind, which can range from yellow to greenish black, is covered with a braided pattern. In Spain, Manchego is a favorite tapa, or small dish, served on its own with sherry or red wine. Italian pecorino romano can be substituted.

CHERRY TOMATO HALVES
WITH SAFFRON AIOLI

To make the saffron aioli, put the lemon juice in a small saucer and warm for several seconds in a microwave. Add the saffron threads, making sure they are all submerged. Set aside.

In a food processor, combine the egg, mustard, and ¾ teaspoon salt. Process to blend. Combine the canola and olive oils in a measuring cup with a lip. With the motor running, start pouring the oil into the food processor in a very thin, slow stream. Continue adding the oil very slowly until about half of the oil has been blended into the egg mixture. With the motor still running, add the remaining oil just a little bit more quickly. Add the saffron lemon juice to the egg mixture, using a small rubber spatula to scrape out all the colored liquid from the saucer. Pulse several times to distribute the saffron in the aioli.

Using the small end of a melon baller, scoop out and discard the seeds from each tomato half. Put the aioli in a squeeze bottle or in a pastry (piping) bag fitted with a ⅜-inch (1-cm) plain or star tip (see page 21). Place the empty tomato shells on a platter and squeeze a teaspoon of the aioli inside each one, decoratively mounding it up over the rim.

Note: This hors d'oeuvre contains raw egg; for more information, see page 112.

Variation Tip: For another flavored aioli, omit the saffron and add ½ teaspoon of best-quality curry powder along with the egg.

MAKES 50 ROOM-TEMPERATURE BITES

FOR THE SAFFRON AIOLI:

1 tablespoon fresh lemon juice

Pinch of saffron threads (about 12 strands)

1 egg, at room temperature

½ teaspoon Dijon mustard

Salt

¾ cup (6 fl oz/180 ml) canola oil

¼ cup (2 fl oz/60 ml) extra-virgin olive oil

25 cherry tomatoes, halved through the stem end

SAFFRON

One of the most distinctive of all seasonings, saffron is highly aromatic and tints food a bright yellow. It is the stigma of a small crocus, and it takes thousands of the tiny threads to make just 1 ounce (30 g) of the spice. Buy saffron threads in small quantities and store them in a cool dark place. Crush the threads only as you need them; powdered saffron loses its flavor more quickly than do the threads.

ELEGANT BITES

A good appetizer should appeal both to the eye and to the sense of taste, and each of the hors d'oeuvres in this chapter meets that double requirement with sophistication and style. They all offer an inviting display of colors and shapes to stimulate the appetite and pleasing contrasts in flavor and texture to amuse the palate.

FILO-WRAPPED FIGS
WITH PERNOD MASCARPONE

Preheat the oven to 350°F (180°C). Line a baking sheet with parchment (baking) paper. Cut each fig lengthwise through the stem end about three-fourths of the way through the fruit. Pull the fig open with your fingers to make a nice large pocket for the filling, being careful not to pull the halves apart.

In a bowl, whisk together the mascarpone, Pernod, and allspice.

Working with 1 filo sheet at a time, and keeping the others covered with a damp towel, place it on a dry work surface and brush it lightly but evenly with olive oil. Place a fig in the center and fill the pocket with about 1½ teaspoons of the mascarpone mixture (there is no need to try to close the fig). Draw up the edges of the filo and pinch firmly above the top of the fig to make a purse shape. Transfer to the lined baking sheet. Repeat with the remaining figs and filo. You should have 16 packets in all.

Bake the packets until golden brown, 10–12 minutes. Transfer each packet to a small plate (see Notes). If desired, tie a chive length around the neck of each purse. Serve warm.

Notes: Plump, pale dried figs can be substituted for the fresh figs. Remove the stems, then place the figs in a large measuring pitcher. Warm 1 cup (8 fl oz/250 ml) dry vermouth or white wine over low heat and pour over the figs. Add warm water as needed to cover the figs completely and let soak for 2 hours. Drain and proceed as directed. Serve these filo packets on small plates with forks, as they are too crumbly to be finger food.

Make-Ahead Tip: These filo fig packets can be refrigerated for up to 4 hours before baking. Bake them straight from the refrigerator, adding 1–2 minutes to the cooking time.

MAKES 16 WARM BITES

16 figs, stems removed

½ cup (4 oz/125 g) mascarpone cheese

1½ teaspoons Pernod, anisette, or other licorice-flavored liqueur

⅛ teaspoon ground allspice

4 sheets filo dough, thawed and quartered (7-by-9-inch/18-by-23-cm pieces)

⅓ cup (3 fl oz/80 ml) olive oil

16 lengths fresh chive (optional)

CHINESE DUCK PARCELS
IN RICE PAPER

FOR THE FILLING:

1¾ lb (875 g) boneless
duck breasts

1 cup (8 fl oz/250 ml) dry
red wine

½ cup (4 fl oz/125 ml)
chicken stock

5 large cloves garlic

20 peppercorns, lightly
crushed

Sea salt

15 or 16 rice paper rounds

¾ English (hothouse)
cucumber, halved and cut
into julienne 1½ inches
(4 cm) long by ¼ inch
(6 mm) thick

2 large shallots, halved and
thinly sliced lengthwise

⅓ cup (3 fl oz/80 ml)
hoisin sauce

To make the filling, in a heavy nonaluminum pan, combine the duck breasts, wine, stock, garlic, peppercorns, and 1 teaspoon salt. Bring to a simmer over medium heat, cover, adjust the heat to maintain a very gentle simmer, and cook until the duck is tender, about 1½ hours. By the end of cooking, most of the duck fat will have been rendered and the duck will be simmering in its own fat. Transfer the duck to a platter lined with paper towels and let cool slightly. Remove and discard the skin and cut the duck meat into strips about 1½ inches (4 cm) long by ½ inch (12 mm) thick.

Have ready on a work surface a large, shallow bowl filled with water and a damp kitchen towel. Immerse a round of rice paper in the water for about 2 seconds, then remove it and spread it on the towel. It will become pliable within a few seconds. Place a few strips of duck, a few cucumber juliennes, and a few slices of shallot in a line across the center of the rice paper, leaving a 2-inch (5-cm) border on either side. Drizzle about 1 teaspoon of the hoisin sauce over the ingredients. Roll the nearest edge up to cover the filling, compacting it gently. Fold in both sides and continue rolling up gently but firmly to the end. Place seam side down on a large platter. Repeat with the remaining ingredients until you have made about 15 rolls. Cover the rolls with the damp towel and set aside until serving time (not more than 2 hours).

To serve, using a sharp knife, cut each roll in half on the diagonal. Arrange on a serving platter and serve.

Note: Hoisin sauce can be found in the ethnic-foods aisle of the supermarket.

MAKES ABOUT 30 ROOM-TEMPERATURE BITES

RICE PAPER
Rice paper is sold in South-east Asian markets in rounds and triangles, packaged in cellophane. Keep unused papers inside a zippered plastic bag and plan to use them up fairly soon after purchase, as they will yellow and become brittle over time. When dipping them into water to soften them, do not allow them to become pliable in the water, or they become hope-lessly flimsy and impossible to manipulate. Always have several extra on hand, in case any should tear in rolling.

OYSTERS WITH A
GARLIC-TARRAGON CRUST

SHUCKING OYSTERS
To shuck oysters, use a folded
cloth to hold the oyster in
your nondominant hand with
the flat top shell facing up.
Holding an oyster knife in your
other hand, insert its tip into
the dark, rounded spot at the
oyster's hinge. Twist the knife
sharply to break the hinge.
Run the knife carefully along
the inside surface of the top
shell, severing the muscle
that grips it. Take care not to
cut the oyster or to spill its
liquor. Discard the top shell.
Carefully cut the muscle under
the oyster to loosen it from
the bottom shell.

Using a mini food processor, with the motor running, drop the garlic cloves through the feed tube. When they are finely minced, add the tarragon and process until minced and combined with the garlic. Add about two-thirds of the bread and process until crumbly. Add the butter, minced celery, ½ teaspoon salt, and ¼ teaspoon pepper and process until well combined. (If not using a processor, mince the garlic cloves and tarragon and place in a bowl. Crumble the bread into fine crumbs and add two-thirds to the bowl along with the butter, minced celery, salt, and pepper. Mix with a fork until well combined.)

Preheat the broiler (grill). Pour the coarse salt into a large, shallow flameproof baking dish, making an even layer about ½ inch (12 mm) thick to serve as a bed for the oysters.

Smear about 1½ teaspoons of the tarragon mixture on top of each oyster. Then, rubbing the reserved bread between your fingers, top each oyster with a dusting of bread crumbs. Nestle the oyster shells in the salt, keeping them as level as possible.

Place the baking dish under the broiler about 4 inches (10 cm) from the heat source and broil (grill) until the topping is bubbling at the edges and beginning to brown, 4–5 minutes. Serve at once.

Note: Celery is too fibrous for the food processor, so it will have to be minced by hand.

MAKES 16 WARM BITES

2 cloves garlic

2 tablespoons chopped
fresh tarragon

1 large slice coarse
country bread, crusts
removed and bread broken
into small pieces

¼ cup (2 oz/60 g)
unsalted butter, at room
temperature

1 celery stalk, minced

Salt and freshly ground
pepper

2–3 cups (1–1½ lb/
500–750 g) coarse salt

16 small oysters, such as
Kumamotos, shucked and
on the half shell *(far left)*

CREMINI MUSHROOMS
STUFFED WITH SPANISH HAM

42 fresh cremini or white button mushrooms, each 2–3 inches (5–7.5 cm) in diameter, brushed clean

2 tablespoons fresh bread crumbs (page 90)

2 tablespoons chopped fresh flat-leaf (Italian) parsley

1 teaspoon minced fresh sage

1 large clove garlic, finely chopped

3 oz (90 g) serrano ham or prosciutto, finely chopped

3 tablespoons crème fraîche or sour cream, or as needed

Salt and freshly ground pepper

2 tablespoons dry white wine or vermouth

2 tablespoons grated Parmesan cheese, plus extra for garnish

Preheat the oven to 400°F (200°C). Lightly oil a heavy baking dish or two large enough to accommodate the mushrooms snugly in a single layer.

Trim off the rough base of each mushroom stem, then remove the stems and chop finely. In a large bowl, combine the chopped stems, the bread crumbs, parsley, sage, garlic, ham, 3 tablespoons crème fraîche, ½ teaspoon salt, and ¼ teaspoon pepper. Mix together thoroughly. The mixture should hold together in clumps. If it seems dry, mix in another teaspoon or two of crème fraîche.

Put the mushroom caps stem sides up in a steamer basket set over simmering water. Cover and steam until tender and glossy, about 3 minutes. Lift out the basket, allowing any moisture to drain, and let cool.

Spoon a generous teaspoon of the ham mixture onto the stem side of each mushroom cap and smooth it into an even, rounded mound. Place the mushrooms, stuffing side up, in the prepared baking dish. Drizzle the wine around the edges of the dish, and sprinkle each cap with about ⅛ teaspoon of the Parmesan.

Bake uncovered until golden, about 30 minutes. Let cool for 5 minutes and serve warm or at room temperature, garnished with Parmesan.

Note: Steaming the mushrooms helps to rid them of excess moisture, creating a more concentrated mushroom flavor. Don't be surprised by how much they shrink, as they have a high moisture content.

Make-Ahead Tip: The steamed mushrooms and stuffing can be stored separately in the refrigerator for up to 24 hours before stuffing.

MAKES 42 WARM OR ROOM-TEMPERATURE BITES

SPANISH HAM

Spanish serrano ham, like its more famous Italian cousin prosciutto, is salted and hung in drying halls to air-cure. It is made primarily in western Spain and is one of the country's classic tapas offerings. Traditionally cut thicker than prosciutto, serrano has a similar but more earthy flavor, in part derived from the sizable role acorns play in the pigs' diet. Although not as widely available as prosciutto, serrano ham is turning up more frequently in delicatessens and specialty-food stores.

51

SMOKED SALMON ROULADES

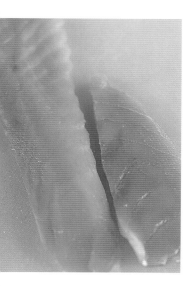

In a food processor, combine ¼ cup (2 oz/60 g) of the salmon trimmings and the butter. Process just until blended, scraping down the bowl sides.

In a small saucepan, combine the clam juice and gelatin. Let stand for 5 minutes. Place the pan over low heat and stir just until the gelatin dissolves. Remove from the heat and stir in the Tabasco and Worcestershire sauces. Pour into the food processor with the salmon mixture and pulse 3 or 4 times, just to blend with the salmon mixture. Transfer to a large bowl.

Whip the cream until stiff. Add one-third of the whipped cream to the salmon mixture and fold together gently. Gently fold in the remaining cream just until no streaks remain. Cover and refrigerate for 10 minutes to allow the gelatin to begin setting.

Place a piece of plastic wrap slightly larger than a salmon rectangle on a work surface, and place a salmon rectangle on top, long side facing you. Patch with trimmings, if necessary, to make the correct-sized rectangle. (Don't worry if there are a few gaps; these may be concealed with the caviar garnish.) Spoon about 3 tablespoons of the salmon mousse lengthwise across the center of the salmon. Using the plastic wrap, pull the edge of the salmon nearest you up and over the mousse and down in the back to meet the other edge. Twist the ends of the plastic to seal and pat into an even log. Repeat with the remaining ingredients to make 5 more rolls. Place all the rolls in the freezer for about 2 hours.

Remove from the freezer and let stand for 10 minutes. Remove the plastic and trim off the untidy ends. Slice the salmon rolls into rounds ¾ inch (2 cm) thick and place on a platter. Let stand for 5–10 minutes to complete the thawing. Place a generous ¼ teaspoon of the tobiko near the edge of each round and serve.

MAKES ABOUT 32 COLD BITES

TRIMMING SALMON

Trimming the salmon for this dish is not an exact science. In a perfect world you would have 6 rectangles exactly the same size, but in fact you may need to patch the rectangles to approximate the size specified. The finished rolls will still look good. (If the salmon pieces are thick, you can pound them gently with a meat mallet or rolling pin to make them thinner and larger.)
As you trim, reserve a few good-sized pieces of fish for possible patching, but set aside about ¼ cup (2 oz/60 g) of the smaller pieces for the salmon mousse.

About 14 oz (440 g) thinly sliced smoked salmon, trimmed on wax paper into 6 rectangles, each 6½ by 3½ inches (16½ by 9 cm), trimmings reserved *(far left)*

2 teaspoons unsalted butter, at room temperature

¼ cup (2 fl oz/60 ml) bottled clam juice or fish stock

1½ teaspoons powdered gelatin

2 drops Tabasco or other hot-pepper sauce

1 drop Worcestershire sauce

½ cup (4 fl oz/125 ml) chilled heavy (double) cream

3 tablespoons wasabi tobiko or salmon roe (page 67)

TUNA TARTARE
ON RUFFLED POTATO CHIPS

FOR THE DRESSING:

1 egg yolk

¾ teaspoon peeled and grated fresh ginger

½ small clove garlic, finely chopped

1½ teaspoons Japanese prepared hot mustard or 1 teaspoon Asian dry hot mustard (see Notes)

1 tablespoon mirin

1 tablespoon soy sauce

¼ cup (2 fl oz/60 ml) rice vinegar

Generous ⅓ cup (3 fl oz/ 80 ml) peanut oil

2 tablespoons Asian sesame oil

¾ lb (375 g) sushi-grade ahi tuna fillet, cut into ⅛-inch (3-mm) dice

2 shallots, finely chopped

2 tablespoons snipped fresh chives, plus sixty 2-inch (5-cm) long pieces

Salt and ground pepper

30 ruffled potato chips, preferably unbroken (see Notes)

To make the dressing, in a food processor, combine the egg yolk, ginger, garlic, mustard, mirin, and soy sauce. Process until smooth, stopping to scrape down the sides of the bowl as necessary. Add the vinegar and process for a few seconds to combine. With the motor running, very slowly drizzle in the peanut and sesame oils just until emulsified, or blended. Transfer to a bowl, cover, and refrigerate until ready to serve.

In a bowl, toss together the tuna, shallots, snipped chives, ½ teaspoon salt, and ½ teaspoon pepper. Add enough of the dressing to moisten the mixture thoroughly and toss again. Do not add so much that the mixture is soupy, however. Reserve any remaining dressing for a green salad.

Arrange the potato chips on a large platter and scoop a generous dollop of tuna tartare onto each chip. Gently press 2 crisscrossed chives into the top of the tartare mixture on each chip and serve at once.

Notes: Japanese hot mustard is sold in small tubes, while Asian dry hot mustard is usually packed in small tins or cellophane packets. Look for these mustards and mirin, or Japanese sweet rice wine, in Asian markets and well-stocked food stores. For the potato chips, use tube-packed ones, which are typically very good and arrive unbroken. This recipe uses raw egg; for more information, see page 112.

Make-Ahead Tips: The dressing can be made up to 2 days in advance of serving and refrigerated. The dressed tuna is best served immediately, but it can be covered and refrigerated for up to 30 minutes.

MAKES ABOUT 30 ROOM-TEMPERATURE OR COLD BITES

TUNA

Tuna is found in many forms, from the canned albacore used for tuna salad to the seared tuna steak served in restaurants. For this dish, however, you must buy only so-called sushi-grade or sashimi-grade tuna, the fish typically used by Japanese chefs for their raw tuna preparations. It is inspected more strictly for freshness than is fish destined for the stove. To ensure the best fish possible, tell your fishmonger that you will be serving the tuna raw, and prepare it on the day of purchase.

TINY ROQUEFORT POPOVERS

POPOVER SAVVY

Most recipes call for pricking popovers as soon as they come out of the oven, to prevent them from becoming soggy. These light and lacy popovers won't need it. You will need 1 or 2 mini popover or muffin pans with a nonstick finish, however, to be sure the popovers are easily freed from the cups. As noted in the recipe, you can reheat them, but do not refrigerate, or they will become irreversibly soggy.

Position an oven rack in the bottom third of the oven and preheat to 450°F (220°C). Generously brush two 12-cup nonstick mini popover or muffin pans with vegetable oil.

In a large bowl, whisk together the flour, salt, white pepper, and parsley. In a large measuring pitcher, whisk together the milk, eggs, and melted butter. Pour the wet ingredients over the dry ingredients and whisk together until just combined (don't worry if a few lumps remain). Pour the batter into the prepared popover cups to within about ¼ inch (6 mm) of the rim (about 1½ table-spoons each). Place a scant teaspoon crumbled cheese in the center of each filled cup.

Bake for 10 minutes. Do not open the oven door during this time. Reduce the heat to 350°F (180°C) and continue to bake until brown and crusty and fully puffed, 8–10 minutes longer.

Remove from the oven and immediately transfer to a warmed platter or napkin-lined bowl. Serve at once. Or, let cool on racks for up to 2 hours, then reheat in a 350°F (180°C) oven for 10 minutes.

MAKES 24 WARM BITES

Vegetable oil, for brushing

1 cup (5 oz / 155 g) all-purpose (plain) flour

½ teaspoon salt

¼ teaspoon freshly ground white pepper

1 tablespoon finely chopped fresh flat-leaf (Italian) parsley

1¼ cups (10 fl oz / 310 ml) milk, at room temperature

2 eggs, at room temperature

1 tablespoon unsalted butter, melted

3 oz (90 g) Roquefort or other strong-flavored, crumbly blue cheese, crumbled

CANAPÉS

For as long as people have gathered together for parties and feasts, canapés—bread or pastry topped with various delicacies—have been among the offerings. The bread may be white, pumpernickel, French, or Italian. The pastry may be puff, short crust, or cheese flavored. Toppings may be as elegant and simple as caviar or as rich and complex as a mushroom ragout.

PROVENÇAL TOASTS

Put the potatoes in a steamer basket over simmering water, cover, and steam until tender, about 5 minutes. Transfer to a bowl.

Preheat a broiler (grill). Brush both sides of the tuna steak with olive oil, then season generously with salt and pepper. Place on a broiler pan and place under the broiler about 4 inches (10 cm) from the heat source. Broil (grill), turning once, until just opaque throughout, about 6 minutes on each side. Transfer to a plate and let cool.

Soak the anchovy fillets in warm water to cover for 5 minutes. Drain, pat dry, and mince.

In a large sauté pan over medium-low heat, warm the 2 tablespoons olive oil. Add the onion, stir to coat with oil, and cover the pan. Cook gently, stirring infrequently, until very soft, about 20 minutes. Add the garlic, anchovies, tomatoes, bay leaves, and chopped oregano. Cover and simmer for 5 minutes. Stir in the tomato paste, capers, vinegar, olives, and potatoes and cook, uncovered, until slightly thickened, about 5 minutes more.

Preheat the broiler again if needed. Cut the tuna into generous ¼-inch (6-mm) chunks and stir into the tomato mixture. Remove from the heat and let stand while you toast the bread.

Cut the bread slices into quarters and lightly brush both sides of each piece with olive oil. Arrange on a broiler pan and place about 4 inches (10 cm) from the heat source. Toast, turning once, until golden, 4–5 minutes on each side.

Arrange the toast quarters on a large platter. Remove the bay leaves from the tuna mixture and top each toast quarter with about 2 tablespoons of the mixture. Garnish with the oregano sprigs and serve at once.

MAKES 32 WARM OR ROOM-TEMPERATURE CANAPÉS

4 small red or Yellow Finn potatoes, unpeeled, cut into scant ½-inch (12-mm) dice

1 ahi tuna steak, 10–12 oz (315–375 g)

2 tablespoons olive oil, plus extra for brushing

Salt and freshly ground pepper

6 anchovy fillets

1 yellow onion, coarsely chopped

3 cloves garlic, minced

6 plum (Roma) tomatoes, seeded and diced

2 bay leaves

1 teaspoon chopped fresh oregano, plus small sprigs for garnish

1 can (6 oz/185 g) tomato paste

¼ cup (2 oz/60 g) capers, rinsed

¼ cup (2 fl oz/60 ml) white wine vinegar

¼ cup (1½ oz/45 g) Niçoise or other brine-cured black olives, pitted and quartered

8 large, thick slices coarse country bread

OPEN-FACED SANDWICHES
OF HERRING, APPLE, AND CHIVES

FOR THE HERRING SALAD:

¾ lb (375 g) pickled herring in sour cream sauce, finely chopped

1 tart apple such as Granny Smith, peeled, cored, and finely chopped

2 tablespoons minced yellow onion

2 tablespoons mayonnaise

Salt and freshly ground white pepper

1 or 2 heads butter lettuce

22 slices cocktail-sized pumpernickel bread

¼ lb (125 g) pickled herring in wine, cut into neat ¼-inch (6-mm) dice

1 small bunch fresh chives, snipped into 1-inch (2.5-cm) lengths

Paprika

To make the herring salad, in a bowl, combine the chopped herring in sour cream, apple, onion, mayonnaise, ¼ teaspoon salt, and ⅛ teaspoon white pepper. Mix well, then taste and adjust the seasoning.

Remove the outer leaves of a butter lettuce head and reserve for salad or another use. Sort through the pale leaves of the heart to find 22 small concave pieces, or "cups." Each cup should be about 1 inch (2.5 cm) wide. If you cannot find enough cups, use the second head.

Begin assembling the canapés. Spread about 1 tablespoon of the herring salad on each pumpernickel slice and place a small butter lettuce cup on the top, pressing it slightly into the salad to make it stick. Place a scant teaspoon of the diced herring in wine inside each cup. Garnish with chive lengths. Continue making canapés until you have used all the ingredients. Scatter a few grains of paprika over each one, place on a platter, and serve at once.

Make-Ahead Tip: The herring salad can be covered and refrigerated for up to 4 hours before stuffing the lettuce cups. It is delicious served chilled.

MAKES 22 ROOM-TEMPERATURE OR COLD CANAPÉS

HERRING

Before refrigeration, this Scandinavian staple fish was necessarily pickled or brined, which led to many wonderful flavor variations. You'll find the fish in food stores and specialty markets in a variety of forms, including the two used here: pickled in wine and cloaked in sour cream. Through the judicious use of colorful vegetables, dark pumpernickel, and careful cutting and presentation, this recipe transforms the humble herring into a culinary star.

PUFF PASTRY PISSALADIÈRES

USING PUFF PASTRY

This miniature version of the traditional Provençal pizza replaces traditional pizza dough with buttery, satisfying, and easy-to-use puff pastry. Frozen puff pastry is an excellent resource. Making the pastry from scratch, which involves careful folding, rolling, and waiting, can be a time-consuming chore for the modern cook. Follow the package instructions as to whether the frozen dough is prerolled or needs additional rolling as described in the recipe.

In a large frying pan over medium-low heat, warm the olive oil. Add the onions, sprinkle with 1 teaspoon salt, ¾ teaspoon pepper, and the thyme, and stir together. Cover and cook very gently until tender, about 45 minutes. Resist the urge to stir too often; a steamy environment is crucial. Uncover the pan and continue to cook gently, now stirring occasionally, until all the excess moisture has evaporated and the mixture resembles a thick jam, about 30 minutes longer.

Preheat the oven to 425°F (220°C). Line a large baking sheet with parchment (baking) paper. On a lightly floured work surface, roll out the puff pastry ⅛ inch (3 mm) thick, taking care not to crush the edges too much with the rolling pin. Using a long, sharp knife, cut into 4-by-1½-inch (10-by-4-cm) rectangles. You should have 42 pieces. If using prerolled frozen puff pastry, which is usually packed 2 sheets to each package, unfold each sheet and, using the fold lines as a guide, cut lengthwise into 3 long rectangles. Then cut each rectangle crosswise at 1½-inch (4-cm) intervals to make 42 pieces.

Place the rectangles on the lined baking sheet, close together but not quite touching. Brush each with a little of the egg mixture. Spread a heaping teaspoon of the onion mixture over each pastry rectangle. Lay an anchovy strip down the center and place an olive quarter at each end of the strip.

Bake until the edges are golden brown, 12–15 minutes. Transfer to a napkin-lined platter or bowl and serve at once. The canapés are also very good served at room temperature, after 30 minutes.

Note: If doubling this recipe, use only 1½ times the amount of salt, not double the amount.

MAKES 42 WARM OR ROOM-TEMPERATURE CANAPÉS

¼ cup (2 fl oz/60 ml) olive oil

3 lb (1.5 kg) mild yellow or sweet onions, halved and sliced paper-thin

Salt and freshly ground pepper (see Note)

1 teaspoon fresh thyme leaves or ½ teaspoon dried thyme

1 package (17 oz/530 g) frozen puff pastry, removed from packaging and thawed for 30 minutes at room temperature

1 egg, lightly beaten with 1 tablespoon water and small pinch of salt

21 anchovy fillets, soaked for 5 minutes in lukewarm water, drained, patted dry, and halved lengthwise

21 Niçoise or other brine-cured black olives, pitted and quartered

PEA BLINI WITH THREE CAVIARS

FOR THE BLINI BATTER:

2½ teaspoons (1 package) quick-rise yeast

1 cup (8 fl oz/250 ml) milk, heated to 110°F (43°C)

1¼ cups (6½ oz/200 g) all-purpose (plain) flour

2 eggs, separated

1 cup (5 oz/155 g) frozen petite peas, thawed

¼ cup (2 fl oz/60 ml) cold milk

About ¼ cup (2 oz/60 g) unsalted butter

1 cup (8 oz/250 g) crème fraîche or sour cream

4 oz (125 g) wasabi tobiko (far right)

4 oz (125 g) golden white-fish caviar

4 oz (125 g) salmon roe

To make the blini batter, in a bowl, combine the yeast, warm milk, flour, and egg yolks. Stir together to blend and then whisk until smooth. Cover the bowl with a kitchen towel and let the batter rise in a warm place until doubled in bulk, 1½–2 hours.

While the batter is rising, in a food processor, combine the peas and cold milk and process, stopping to scrape down the sides of the bowl as necessary, until very smooth, 1–2 minutes.

Add the pea purée to the batter and stir until thoroughly combined. Re-cover the bowl and let the batter rise until very spongy in appearance, about 1 hour longer.

In a large, perfectly clean bowl, beat the egg whites with an electric mixer or whisk until stiff peaks form. Fold into the batter.

In a large nonstick frying pan over low heat, melt about 2 teaspoons of the butter. Ladle about 2 tablespoons of the batter into the pan for each blini, being careful not to crowd the pan. Cook until the bottoms are lightly browned and bubbles have formed on the top, about 3 minutes. Flip the blini over and cook until browned on the second sides, about 2 minutes longer. Transfer to a warmed platter, cover with aluminum foil, and place in a low oven. Cook the remaining blini in the same way, adding butter to the pan as needed. You should have about 48 blini in all. The blini can remain in a low (200°F/95°C) oven for up to 30 minutes before topping.

To serve, spread about 1 teaspoon crème fraîche over the top of each blini. Top each blini with a scant ½ teaspoon of one of the caviars or a mixture of all three. Serve at once.

Variation Tip: To make plain blini, omit the peas and cold milk and increase the amount of warm milk by ¼ cup (2 fl oz/60 ml). Top with black caviar if desired.

MAKES ABOUT 48 WARM CANAPÉS

COLORFUL CAVIARS

Caviar, a term that in its strictest usage refers only to the roe (eggs) of various members of the sturgeon family, is no longer restricted to the traditional beluga, osetra, and sevruga varieties. North American golden whitefish caviar is getting good reviews. Stunning orange tobiko, flying fish roe that is sometimes colored green with wasabi, a Japanese horseradish-like root, is a fine choice as well. Glistening orange, large-sized salmon roe also makes a dramatic statement.

STEAK TARTARE ON BAGUETTE CROÛTES

To make the *croûtes,* preheat the oven to 375°F (190°C). Brush or spray 1 side of the bread slices lightly with the olive oil. Sprinkle the oiled side with a little pepper and place oiled side up on a baking sheet. Bake until just golden, 10–12 minutes. Transfer to a platter or tray and let cool.

To make the steak tartare, place the filet mignon in the freezer for 20 minutes to firm it. In a large bowl, combine the onion, capers, lime juice, Worcestershire sauce, extra-virgin olive oil, and Tabasco sauce. Mix well, cover, and refrigerate.

On a very clean cutting board, cut the beef into about ¼-inch (6-mm) dice. Put the dice in a food processor and pulse quickly 6–8 times, until the beef is ground (minced) but not pulverized. Add the beef to the bowl containing the onion mixture and mix together quickly but thoroughly with a fork.

Top each *croûte* with a large spoonful of steak tartare and scatter with the mint. Serve immediately, while the beef is still chilled.

Note: This dish is based on raw beef. If you choose to serve beef raw, be sure to buy the meat from a reputable butcher who is able to answer any questions you have about it. For more information, see page 111.

Make-Ahead Tips: The croûtes *can be prepared up to 1 hour in advance and set aside. Or, place the cooled* croûtes *in an airtight container and store at room temperature overnight. The beef mixture can be covered and refrigerated before topping the* croûtes, *but for no more than 30 minutes.*

MAKES 25 COLD CANAPÉS

FOR THE CROÛTES:

25 baguette slices, ¼–½ inch (6–12 mm) thick

Olive oil or nonstick olive-oil cooking spray

Freshly ground pepper

½ lb (250 g) filet mignon, trimmed of all fat and gristle (see Note)

¼ cup (2 oz/60 g) minced white onion

¼ cup (2 oz/60 g) capers, rinsed and finely chopped

1 tablespoon fresh lime juice

1 teaspoon Worcestershire sauce

1 teaspoon extra-virgin olive oil

Dash of Tabasco or other hot-pepper sauce

2 tablespoons finely chopped fresh mint or flat-leaf (Italian) parsley

GOAT CHEESE CRISPS
WITH MUSHROOM RAGOUT

FOR THE CRISPS:

⅔ cup (3½ oz/105 g)
all-purpose (plain) flour

3 tablespoons unsalted
butter, at room temperature

5 oz (155 g) fresh goat
cheese, at room temperature

3 tablespoons crème fraîche
or sour cream

Salt

FOR THE RAGOUT:

1 lb (500 g) assorted fresh
mushrooms such as cremini,
oyster, shiitake, and white
button, brushed clean
(far right)

1 tablespoon unsalted butter

1 tablespoon olive oil

1 large shallot, finely
chopped

2 cloves garlic, minced

2 tablespoons Madeira or
dry sherry

1 tablespoon heavy (double)
cream (optional)

Salt and ground pepper

1 egg white

Chopped fresh dill for garnish

To make the crisps, in a food processor, combine the flour, butter, goat cheese, crème fraîche, and 1 teaspoon salt. Process until the mixture appears crumbly. Turn out onto a board and work together with your hands to form a log about 8 inches (20 cm) long and 1½ inches (4 cm) in diameter. Wrap with plastic wrap and refrigerate for at least 1 hour.

To make the ragout, cut all of the mushrooms into ¼-inch (6-mm) pieces. In a large frying pan over medium heat, melt the butter with the olive oil. Add the shallot and sauté until it begins to soften, about 2 minutes. Add the mushrooms and cook, stirring occasionally, until softened and almost dry, about 7 minutes. Add the garlic and cook for 1 minute longer. Pour in the Madeira and simmer until completely reduced, about 2 minutes. Stir in the cream, if using, and ½ teaspoon salt, then remove from the heat. Add a pinch of pepper and taste for seasoning. The mixture should be very thick. Cover to keep warm.

Preheat the oven to 375°F (190°). Slice the log into rounds ¼ inch (6 mm) thick and place on an ungreased baking sheet. Lightly beat the egg white with a pinch of salt, then brush onto the cheese crisps. Bake until golden, 18–20 minutes. Let cool slightly.

Transfer the warm crisps to a platter and top each crisp with a spoonful of warm ragout. Garnish with dill and serve at once.

Make-Ahead Tip: The cheese log will keep for up to 2 days in the refrigerator before slicing and baking.

Variation Tip: For a quicker dish, prepare the crisps as directed and top them with a dollop of crème fraîche, ½ teaspoon salmon roe, and a small sprig of fresh dill.

MAKES ABOUT 32 WARM CANAPÉS

CLEANING MUSHROOMS

Gently brushing mushrooms with a soft brush or a kitchen towel is preferable to washing them. Porous mushrooms will soak up water like a sponge, compromising both the texture and flavor of any dish. Do not scrub so hard that you remove the thin outer skin on the caps. You want only to loosen any dirt or grit, of which there is usually very little. To speed the cleaning process, rinse the soft brush in cool water in between brushing each mushroom.

POLENTA CROSTINI WITH SAUSAGE TOPPING

Rinse an 8-by-12-inch (20-by-30-cm) baking pan with cold water and shake it dry. Mound the hot polenta in the pan and, using a spatula repeatedly dipped in very hot water, spread the polenta into a layer a little less than ½ inch (12 mm) thick. Cover with a kitchen towel and let rest at room temperature for at least 1 hour.

Heat a large nonstick or cast-iron frying pan over medium heat. Add the sausages and cook, stirring and breaking up the meat, until no trace of pink remains, 5–7 minutes. Using a slotted spoon, transfer the sausage to a double thickness of paper towels to drain. Discard any fat from the pan and wipe out with a paper towel.

Return the pan to medium heat and warm the olive oil. Add the onion and garlic and sauté them until softened, about 5 minutes. Add the tomatoes, bay leaf, ½ teaspoon salt, and ¼ teaspoon pepper and bring to a simmer. Cook, stirring occasionally, until the liquid has evaporated and the mixture is quite thick, about 10 minutes. Discard the bay leaf, stir in the cooked sausage and the basil, and keep warm while you brown the polenta.

Preheat the broiler (grill). Cut the polenta into 32 pieces. In batches if necessary, transfer the pieces to a broiler pan and brush the tops with half of the melted butter. Sprinkle with pepper to taste.

Place under the broiler about 3 inches (7.5 cm) from the heat source and broil (grill) until golden and crisp, about 5 minutes. Turn and brush the other sides with the remaining butter and broil until golden, about 4 minutes longer.

Transfer the polenta pieces to a platter and top each with a small dollop of the warm sausage topping. Serve immediately.

MAKES 32 WARM BITES

SOFT POLENTA

In a heavy saucepan over high heat, combine 2 cups (16 fl oz/500 ml) chicken stock, 1 cup (8 fl oz/250 ml) milk, and ¾ teaspoon salt and bring to a boil. Reduce the heat to simmer. Add 1 cup (5 oz/155 g) slow-cooking polenta in a slow, thin stream, whisking constantly. Reduce the heat to very low. Stir vigorously with a wooden spoon every 1–2 minutes until the grains of polenta have softened, 12–15 minutes. Stir in 2 tablespoons butter and ⅓ cup (1½ oz/45 g) grated Parmesan cheese and remove from the heat.

Soft Polenta *(far left)*

2 fresh pork, chicken, or turkey sausages, about ½ lb (250 g) total weight, casings removed

2 tablespoons olive oil

½ small yellow onion, finely chopped

2 large cloves garlic, finely chopped

1 can (14 oz/440 g) diced plum (Roma) tomatoes with juice

1 small bay leaf

Salt and freshly ground pepper

1 tablespoon finely chopped fresh basil

3 tablespoons unsalted butter, melted

DIPS AND SPREADS

Two of the most perennially popular finger food offerings, creamy dips and spreads share an ease of preparation and serving. Set out with trimmed vegetables or chips, bread or crackers, these simple dishes can be the centerpiece of a casual gathering.

BLUE CHEESE DIP
76

GREEN GODDESS DIP
79

PICKLED-GARLIC AIOLI
80

THAI GUACAMOLE
83

EGGPLANT AND GINGER SPREAD
84

SMOKED TROUT MOUSSE
WITH ORANGE AND CHIVES
87

BLUE CHEESE DIP

In a food processor, combine three-fourths of the blue cheese, the sour cream, cream cheese, lemon zest and juice, ¾ teaspoon salt, ¼ teaspoon white pepper, and 1 clove of the garlic. Pulse until well combined but still a little lumpy, stopping to scrape down the sides of the bowl as necessary. Taste and add the second clove of garlic, if desired.

Transfer the dip to a bowl. Stir in most of the the remaining blue cheese with a fork, mashing it up a little, and scatter the rest over the top. Cover and refrigerate for at least 1 hour to allow the flavors to marry. Since chilled mixtures taste less flavorful than room-temperature ones, let this dip stand at room temperature for about 30 minutes before serving.

MAKES 2 CUPS (16 FL OZ/500 ML)

1 cup (5 oz/155 g) crumbled Maytag blue cheese

1 cup (8 oz/250 g) sour cream

¼ lb (125 g) cream cheese, at room temperature

1½ teaspoons minced or grated lemon zest

1 tablespoon fresh lemon juice

Salt and freshly ground white pepper

1 or 2 cloves garlic, minced

CRUDITÉS

Both this dip and Green Goddess Dip (page 79) are superb with crudités, an assortment of raw vegetables trimmed and cut for dipping. Among the possibilities are celery, zucchini (courgette), cucumber, and carrot sticks; jicama and yellow bell pepper (capsicum) strips; and whole or halved radishes and cherry tomatoes. Assemble crudités with an eye toward color and texture. Both dips are also wonderful with a variety of chips.

GREEN GODDESS DIP

3 anchovy fillets

1 green (spring) onion, including tender green parts, finely chopped

2 tablespoons finely chopped fresh flat-leaf (Italian) parsley

1 tablespoon finely chopped fresh tarragon

1 cup (8 fl oz/250 ml) mayonnaise

½ cup (4 oz/125 g) sour cream

1½ tablespoons Champagne vinegar or white wine vinegar

2 tablespoons finely snipped fresh chives

Salt and freshly ground white pepper

Soak the anchovies in warm water for 5 minutes. Drain, pat dry, and mince.

In a food processor, combine the anchovies, green onion, parsley, tarragon, mayonnaise, sour cream, vinegar, chives, ½ teaspoon salt or to taste, and ¼ teaspoon white pepper. Pulse briefly to mix, stopping to scrape down the sides of the bowl as necessary.

Transfer to a bowl, cover, and refrigerate for at least 1 hour to allow the flavors to marry. (The dip will keep in the refrigerator for up to 2 days.) Let stand at room temperature for 30 minutes before serving.

Note: This dip may also be used as a creamy salad dressing over romaine (cos) or iceberg lettuce hearts.

MAKES ABOUT 1¾ CUPS (14 FL OZ/430 ML)

DIP PRESENTATION
Consider forgoing the usual bowl for serving this dip, spooning it instead into a hollowed-out red or green cabbage, a rounded romaine (cos) lettuce or radicchio leaf cup, or even a seeded small pumpkin. Serve with zucchini (courgette) rounds and sliced fennel, carrots, and celery, or other crudités (see page 76).

PICKLED-GARLIC AIOLI

In a food processor, combine the whole egg, egg yolk, vinegar, mustard, and ½ teaspoon salt. Pulse until evenly blended. With the motor running, drizzle in the olive and canola oils very slowly at first, adding them at a slightly faster rate after the first ⅓ cup (3 fl oz/80 ml) or so is emulsified, or thoroughly blended. Add the boiling water and lemon juice and pulse 2 or 3 times. Add the garlic, capers, parsley, and 1 teaspoon pepper and pulse until just blended. The dip should appear slightly chunky.

Transfer to a bowl and refrigerate for at least 1 hour, to allow the flavors to marry. (The dip will keep in the refrigerator for up to 1 day.) Let stand at room temperature for 30 minutes, then give it a sprinkling of pepper before serving.

Note: This dip contains raw egg; for more information, see page 112.

Serving Tip: Serve with Japanese cucumbers, leaves of baby bok choy, long wedges of daikon radish, and/or sesame crackers.

MAKES 2⅓ CUPS (19 FL OZ/590 ML)

PICKLED GARLIC
Pickled garlic is available in jars in Japanese markets and comes in various colors and flavors, such as green seaweed and orange bonito. Any one will be fine for this recipe, and orange bonito is an especially good choice. You can also find pickled garlic at fine food and gourmet stores, through mail-order catalogs, and online.

1 whole egg plus 1 egg yolk

1 tablespoon red wine vinegar

2 teaspoons Dijon mustard

Salt and freshly ground pepper

⅓ cup (3 fl oz/80 ml) olive oil

1 cup (8 fl oz/250 ml) canola oil

1 tablespoon boiling water

2 tablespoons fresh lemon juice

⅓ cup (2½ oz/75 g) Japanese pickled garlic, sliced

3 tablespoons capers, rinsed

1 tablespoon finely chopped fresh flat-leaf (Italian) parsley

THAI GUACAMOLE

4 avocados, pitted and peeled

1 large red bell pepper (capsicum), seeded and diced

5 green (spring) onions, including tender green parts, finely chopped

¼ cup (⅓ oz/10 g) finely chopped fresh mint

1 tablespoon peeled and grated fresh ginger

Tender heart of 1 lemongrass stalk, minced *(far right)* (about 1 tablespoon)

3 tablespoons fresh lime juice

1 tablespoon soy sauce

1 tablespoon Asian fish sauce

½ teaspoon Chinese chile paste with garlic (page 112)

Sea salt

In a large bowl, mash the avocados with a fork until mostly, but not completely, smooth. Stir in the bell pepper, green onions, mint, ginger, lemongrass, lime juice, soy sauce, fish sauce, chile paste, and salt to taste. (The soy sauce and fish sauce are both salty, so taste before adding salt.) Mix thoroughly.

Cover and refrigerate for 1 hour to allow the flavors to marry. Serve at once.

Serving Tip: Serve this dip with red, black, and/or blue tortilla chips.

MAKES ABOUT 2 CUPS (16 FL OZ/500 ML)

LEMONGRASS

This long, slender, fibrous lemon-scented grass native to Asia marries deliciously with the distinctive flavors of Mexico. The coarse, paper-dry upper portion is cut off and discarded, and the bulbous base, usually 3–4 inches (7.5–10 cm) long, is either pounded or thinly sliced to release its fragrance. When cut crosswise, a fine series of concentric rings is revealed. If fresh lemongrass is not available, substitute 1 tablespoon slivered lemon balm or chopped lemon zest. Keep lemongrass for up to 2 weeks in a refrigerator crisper.

EGGPLANT AND GINGER SPREAD

PREPARING EGGPLANT

Ridding eggplants of some moisture often results in a more successful dish. For this spread, the eggplants are roasted and left to drain for at least 30 minutes. Sometimes eggplants are cut, salted, and allowed to drain while still raw, so that less moisture is released in cooking. Smaller eggplants of different varieties contain less moisture than the more typical large globe eggplants and generally do not require salting before cooking. Seek out small globe eggplants for this dish for the best results.

Preheat the oven to 400°F (200°C). Pierce the eggplants in several places with a fork and place in a roasting pan. Roast for 30 minutes. Turn the eggplants over and continue to roast until they are very tender, slightly charred, and the centers have collapsed, about 30 minutes longer. Transfer to a colander set over a large bowl and let drain for at least 30 minutes or up to 2 hours.

Pull off the skin from the eggplants and discard. Squeeze the eggplants gently to extract a little more of the moisture. Cut the eggplant flesh into chunks, removing any seed sacs. In a food processor, combine the eggplant flesh, egg, garlic, ginger, ¾ teaspoon salt, ¼ teaspoon white pepper, and the vinegar. Purée until very smooth, stopping to scrape down the sides of the bowl as necessary. With the motor running, add the olive oil very slowly, processing until the mixture forms a smooth, fluffy paste.

Transfer to a serving bowl and stir in the chopped cilantro. Cover and refrigerate for 1 hour to allow the flavors to marry. Let the dip come to room temperature for 30 minutes before serving. Garnish with cilantro sprigs and serve with pita wedges and celery sticks.

Note: This recipe uses raw egg. For more information, see page 112.

Make-Ahead Tips: The draining eggplants can be placed in the refrigerator, covered with a kitchen towel, and kept overnight. Or, the finished spread will keep in the refrigerator for up to 1 day.

Preparation Tip: To intensify the smoky flavor, char the outside of each eggplant over a gas flame before finishing them in the oven for 30 minutes. It will be more difficult to remove the skin and you will end up with a few flecks of black in the mixture, but the smoky flavor will be delicious.

MAKES ABOUT 2 ½ CUPS (20 FL OZ/625 ML)

2 small globe eggplants (aubergines), about 2¼ lb (1.1 kg) total weight

1 egg

1 large clove garlic, finely chopped

1 tablespoon peeled and grated fresh ginger (about 1½-inch/4-cm length)

Salt and freshly ground white pepper

½ teaspoon white wine vinegar

⅔ cup (5 fl oz/160 ml) extra-virgin olive oil

1 tablespoon finely chopped fresh cilantro (fresh coriander), plus sprigs for garnish

5 pita bread rounds, each cut into 8 wedges

Celery sticks for serving

SMOKED TROUT MOUSSE WITH ORANGE AND CHIVES

1¼ cups (10 oz/315 g)
fromage blanc or quark
(see Note)

3 oz (90 g) cream cheese,
at room temperature

3 large cloves garlic, finely
chopped

Salt

Pinch of cayenne pepper

¼ lb (125 g) smoked trout
fillet, skinned and coarsely
chopped

Finely shredded zest of
2 oranges

2 tablespoons snipped
fresh chives, plus 1-inch
(2.5-cm) lengths for garnish

35 cracked-pepper water
biscuits or cocktail-sized
pumpernickel bread slices

In a food processor, combine the fromage blanc, cream cheese, garlic, ½ teaspoon salt, and cayenne. Process until smooth. Add the smoked trout and half of the orange zest and pulse a few times just to combine.

Transfer to a bowl and gently stir in the snipped chives. Cover and chill in the refrigerator for at least 2 hours or up to 4 hours.

Scoop the mousse into small soufflé dishes, or other serving bowls. Let come to room temperature for 30 minutes before serving. Scatter the remaining orange zest and the chive lengths over the top of the mousse and serve with the water biscuits.

Note: Fromage blanc is a French-style fresh cheese made of cow's milk. Quark is the German version. Both are tangy and naturally low in fat and are increasingly available in well-stocked food stores. Small-curd cottage cheese or pot cheese may be substituted. If using the former, whirl briefly in a food processor to refine the texture.

Preparation Tip: For a more pungent spread, double the amount of smoked trout.

MAKES ABOUT 2 CUPS (16 FL OZ/500 ML)

ZESTING CITRUS

For citrus zest, choose organic fruit if possible and be sure to scrub the fruit well to remove any wax or residue. Cut off only the thin, colored portion of the rind, taking care not to include the bitter white pith. You can use a zester, a tool designed to remove the zest in long, thin strips. A vegetable peeler or a paring knife can also be used, but often produces pieces that are short but wide and need further slicing. Zest may be removed with the fine rasps of a handheld grater as well.

WRAPS AND SKEWERS

Whether the wrapping is grape leaves or thin pastry, whether the skewers hold tidbits of meat or seafood, the following recipes will satisfy a hungry crowd without a need for plates or forks—an important consideration for a big stand-up party.

CRISP OYSTER SKEWERS
WITH LEMON BUTTER

Preheat a broiler (grill). Pat the oysters dry with paper towels. Thread 4 oysters (or pieces of larger oysters) onto each of 4 skewers. If using wooden skewers, wrap about 1 inch (2.5 cm) of the blunt end of each skewer with aluminum foil to provide a handle.

In a small bowl or cup, combine the butter and lemon juice and brush the oysters thoroughly with some of the mixture. On a plate, mix together the bread crumbs, lemon zest, minced parsley, curry powder, 1 teaspoon salt, and pepper to taste. Gently roll the skewered oysters back and forth in the crumb mixture and spoon the mixture over the top, to coat them as evenly as possible.

Arrange the skewers on a broiler pan and place under the broiler about 5 inches (13 cm) from the heat source. Broil (grill) on the first side until golden, about 4 minutes. Gently turn the skewers over, using tongs to turn individual oysters completely. Baste with a little more butter mixture, if desired, and broil until the second side is crisp and golden, about 3 minutes longer.

Transfer to a platter and let cool for 1 minute. Decorate the platter with lemon rounds and parsley sprigs, then serve.

Note: If the shucked oysters are more than 1½ inches (4 cm) in diameter, use fewer oysters and cut them into halves or even into quarters. Use the pieces in place of a whole oyster. For instructions on shucking oysters, see page 48.

MAKES 4 WARM SKEWERS

FRESH BREAD CRUMBS

To make fresh bread crumbs, use any bread a few days past its peak of freshness, or lay fresh bread slices flat on a countertop and leave overnight to dry out. Cut off the crusts, tear the slices into bite-sized pieces, then process in a blender or food processor to the desired texture. Store homemade bread crumbs in a zippered plastic bag in the refrigerator for up to 4 days.

16 oysters, shucked
(see Note)

2 tablespoons salted
butter, melted

2 teaspoons fresh lemon
juice

¾ cup (1½ oz/45 g) fresh
bread crumbs, very finely
ground (about 1½ slices
coarse country bread)
(far left)

½ teaspoon minced
lemon zest

1 tablespoon fresh flat-leaf
(Italian) parsley leaves,
minced, plus sprigs
for garnish

½ teaspoon curry powder

Salt and freshly ground
pepper

Lemon rounds for garnish

4 small metal skewers or
wooden cocktail skewers
soaked in water for
20–30 minutes

DEEP-FRIED WONTONS
WITH CREAMY CURRIED CHICKEN

FOR THE FILLING:

3 oz (90 g) cream cheese, at room temperature

Scant 1 teaspoon curry powder

¾ cup (about 5 oz/155 g) diced cooked chicken (¼-inch/6-mm dice)

⅓ cup (1½ oz/45 g) slivered blanched almonds, coarsely chopped

1½ tablespoons heavy (double) cream

1 tablespoon Major Grey or other mango chutney, coarsely chopped

Salt

48 square wonton wrappers

Vegetable oil for deep-frying

15–20 fresh flat-leaf (Italian) parsley sprigs, well dried (optional)

To make the filling, in a bowl, combine the cream cheese and curry powder and beat with a wooden spoon until fluffy. Stir in the chicken, almonds, cream, chutney, and ¼ teaspoon salt until well blended.

Lightly flour a work surface and a baking sheet. Place 1 wonton wrapper on the work surface with a point facing you. Place 1 rounded teaspoon of the filling just below the center of the wrapper. Brush the edges of the wrapper very lightly with water and bring down the top point to meet the bottom, forming a triangle. Press the edges firmly to seal, forcing out any air. Transfer to the baking sheet and cover with a kitchen towel while you make the rest of the wontons.

Pour vegetable oil into a heavy saucepan to a depth of 3 inches (7.5 cm) and heat to 375°F (190°C). Add the wontons, 4 or 5 at a time, and fry until golden, about 1½ minutes. Using tongs or a wire skimmer, transfer to paper towels to drain, then keep warm in a low (200°F/95°C) oven while you fry the remaining wontons. Between each batch, let the oil return to 375°F.

Arrange the wontons on a napkin-lined platter for serving. If desired, fry parsley sprigs in the hot oil until crisp, 10–15 seconds. Drain briefly on paper towels and scatter over the wontons.

Caution: When deep-frying, do not let the oil get too hot. If it reaches a temperature of 400°F (200°C) or beyond, it may burst into flame.

Make-Ahead Tip: The wontons can be refrigerated for up to 6 hours, covered with plastic wrap, before frying. Or, freeze them for up to 1 month. Deep-fry them still frozen; the cooking time will be the same.

MAKES ABOUT 48 WARM BITES

DEEP-FRYING SAVVY

If you do not have a deep-fryer with a built-in thermometer, use a heavy, deep saucepan and a deep-frying thermometer that can be clipped to the side. Never fill the pan more than a third full of oil, and use an oil with a high smoke point, such as safflower, peanut, or canola. Add food in small batches, to prevent a sudden drop in the oil temperature, and use tongs to lower the food into the hot oil, avoiding spatters. Always let the oil return to its correct frying temperature between batches to avoid greasiness.

TEMPURA VEGETABLES

Pour the ¾ cup soda water into a bowl. In a sifter, combine the flour, cornstarch, and 1½ teaspoons salt and sift into the soda water. Whisk until evenly blended. The batter should have the consistency of thin pancake batter. Add a little more soda water if necessary to thin it. Cover and refrigerate for 45–60 minutes.

Push a skewer almost but not quite through the center of each mushroom piece. Push a skewer lengthwise into each zucchini piece, inserting it about halfway into the piece.

Pour vegetable oil into a large, deep saucepan to a depth of about 3 inches (7.5 cm) and heat to 375°F (190°C) on a deep-frying thermometer. Dip a skewered vegetable into the tempura batter, coating it completely and letting the excess batter drip back into the bowl for a moment. Insert it gently into the hot oil, standing the skewer upright against the side of the pan. Immediately batter the next piece and put it in the oil. Repeat until you have 4 pieces in the oil. (Do not fry more than 4 pieces at a time, or the temperature will drop and the vegetables will absorb the oil.) Fry, occasionally moving the pieces slightly to prevent them from sticking to one another and so they will fry evenly on all sides, until the batter is crisp, pale gold, and slightly puffed, about 2 minutes. Transfer each skewer to a paper towel–lined baking pan and keep warm in a low (200°F/95°C) oven while you fry the remaining skewered vegetables. Between each batch, let the oil return to 375°F (190°C) and use a skimmer to remove any bits of batter that remain in the oil, to prevent them from burning. When all of the skewered vegetables are done, use tongs to dip the onion pieces into the batter and fry them in the hot oil in the same way.

Place the bowl of dipping sauce in the center of a large platter and arrange the vegetables around the bowl. Decorate the platter with daikon sprouts, if desired, and serve immediately.

MAKES 40 WARM BITES

SPICY DIPPING SAUCE

Tempura needs a salty, tangy dip to balance its richness. For a classic tempura dipping sauce with a spicy twist, try this mixture. In a small serving bowl, stir together 2 tablespoons sake, 1 tablespoon rice vinegar, 2 teaspoons mirin (Japanese sweet rice wine), 2 teaspoons Asian fish sauce, 2 teaspoons soy sauce, and 1 seeded and minced small hot red or green chile such as Thai, serrano, or Scotch bonnet, if desired. Set aside until serving.

¾ cup (6 fl oz/180 ml) plus 2 tablespoons soda water, or as needed

⅔ cup (3½ oz/105 g) all-purpose (plain) flour

3 tablespoons cornstarch (cornflour)

Salt

8 firm fresh white button mushrooms, each about 2 inches (5 cm) in diameter, stems trimmed flush with the underside, mushrooms halved

1 zucchini (courgette), about 9 inches (23 cm) long, trimmed, quartered lengthwise, and cut into sixteen 2-inch (5-cm) lengths

Vegetable oil for deep-frying

4 green (spring) onions, tough green ends trimmed and onions halved crosswise

Spicy Dipping Sauce (far left), for serving

Daikon radish or alfalfa sprouts for garnish (optional)

32 wooden cocktail skewers soaked in water for 20–30 minutes

LAMB AND ARTICHOKE HEART SPIEDINI

1¼ lb (625 g) lamb from the leg, trimmed of fat and gristle and cut into ¾-inch (2-cm) cubes (see Notes)

1 lb (500 g) frozen artichoke hearts, thawed (see Notes)

Grated zest and juice of 1 lemon, plus lemon wedges for garnish

3 tablespoons olive oil

1 large clove garlic, minced

2 teaspoons finely chopped fresh rosemary, plus sprigs for garnish

Salt and freshly ground pepper

Canola or grapeseed oil, if using griddle

14 metal cocktail skewers or wooden cocktail skewers soaked in water for 20–30 minutes

In a bowl, combine the lamb, artichoke hearts, lemon zest and juice, olive oil, garlic, chopped rosemary, ½ teaspoon salt, and ¼ teaspoon pepper. Toss gently and let stand for 1 hour, or cover and refrigerate for up to 6 hours. Toss the mixture occasionally.

Prepare a fire in a grill, or place a cast-iron griddle over two burners on your stove top, brush it with canola oil, and heat it over medium-high heat.

Thread the ingredients onto each skewer. Position the foods close to the pointed end of the skewer and press the lamb pieces snugly together. If using wooden skewers, wrap about 3 inches (7.5 cm) of the blunt end of each skewer with aluminum foil to provide a handle.

Place the skewers on the grill rack about 6 inches (15 cm) from the heat, or arrange on the preheated griddle. Cook until browned on the first side, about 2½ minutes, then turn and grill until browned on the second side and just firm to the touch, 2–3 minutes longer. The lamb tastes best when medium-rare.

Transfer the skewers to a warmed platter and sprinkle with a little salt. Garnish with rosemary sprigs and lemon wedges and serve.

Notes: Lamb breast and shoulder cuts are too tough for this quick-cooking method. The best choice is to use steaks cut from the leg, as a whole or half boned lamb leg yields too much meat. Do not worry if the artichoke hearts are not completely thawed before they go into the marinade. They will catch up quickly.

MAKES 14 WARM SKEWERS

USING SKEWERS

When threading ingredients onto small cocktail skewers (*spiedini* in Italian), be sure to keep the ingredients close to the pointed end. This creates a handle and makes it easier for guests to consume the 2 or 3 bites without needing a fork to push the speared food to the end. Small metal skewers, about 6 inches (15 cm) long, are great for grilling hors d'oeuvres, but wooden skewers can work well if they are soaked. Be sure to wrap the blunt ends of wooden skewers in foil to prevent them from burning.

VINE LEAVES STUFFED
WITH WILD RICE AND APRICOTS

GRAPE LEAVES

Grape leaves are among
the best wrappers for
hors d'oeuvres. They taste
good, they stand up well to
heat, and brine-packed ones
will keep almost indefinitely.

If fresh grape leaves are
available to you, choose the
largest leaves and parboil
them for 5 minutes in salted
boiling water to make them
pliable enough for wrapping.

Put the spinach, with only the rinsing water clinging to the leaves, in a frying pan. Place over medium-low heat, cover, and cook, tossing once or twice, until just tender, about 5 minutes. Remove from the heat, let cool, squeeze dry, and chop coarsely.

In a bowl, combine the spinach, wild rice, apricots, shallot, ½ teaspoon salt, pepper to taste, and lemon juice. Mix well.

Discard any grape leaves that are too small or damaged and trim the tough stems from the remaining leaves. Place a leaf, vein side up, on a work surface, with the stem end closest to you. Scoop up a generous rounded tablespoon of the rice mixture and press down firmly with the cupped palm of your other hand to compact the filling into an egg shape. Place the filling across the stem end of the vine leaf, ¼ inch (6 mm) from the bottom edge. Fold the stem end up and over the filling, fold in the two sides over the filling, and then, starting at the stem end, roll up into a compact packet. Place the packet, seam side down, in a 12-inch (30-cm) frying pan. Repeat until you have used up all the filling. The packets should fit snugly in the pan.

Drizzle the olive oil and then the chicken stock over the packets and place over medium-low heat. Bring the liquid to a slow simmer and cover the pan. Simmer very gently until the liquid is almost fully absorbed, about 20 minutes. Remove from the heat, uncover the pan, and let cool to room temperature.

Cut the feta cheese into as many cubes as you have packets. When the packets are cool, place a cube of feta on top of each packet and use a cocktail pick to skewer the two together. Transfer to a platter and serve at room temperature.

MAKES 25–30 ROOM-TEMPERATURE BITES

2 packed cups (2½ oz/75 g) stemmed spinach leaves

Scant ½ cup (3 oz/90 g) wild rice, cooked according to package directions

16 dried apricots, plumped in warm water for 20 minutes, drained, and coarsely chopped

1 shallot, finely chopped

Sea salt

Freshly ground pepper

2 teaspoons fresh lemon juice

25–30 brine-packed grape leaves, soaked in very hot water for 30 minutes and drained

3 tablespoons olive oil

½ cup (4 fl oz/125 ml) chicken stock

6 oz (185 g) firm feta cheese

25–30 cocktail picks

PORK PINCHITOS
WITH TOMATO ROMESCO SAUCE

⅓ cup (3 fl oz/80 ml) dry white wine

½ cup (4 fl oz/125 ml) extra-virgin olive oil

3 teaspoons sweet paprika

Salt and pepper

2 cloves garlic, minced

1 bay leaf, crumbled

Pinch of red pepper flakes

1 lb (500 g) lean boneless pork loin

2 slices coarse country bread, crusts removed

3 tablespoons red wine vinegar

⅓ cup (1½ oz/45 g) slivered blanched almonds, toasted *(far right)*

2 plum (Roma) tomatoes, ¼ lb (125 g), peeled and seeded (page 28), then coarsely chopped

Pinch of cayenne pepper

½ lemon

22 small metal skewers or wooden cocktail skewers soaked in water for 20–30 minutes

In a nonaluminum bowl, combine the wine, half of the olive oil, 2 teaspoons of the paprika, 1 teaspoon salt, ¾ teaspoon pepper, 1 minced clove garlic, the bay leaf, and the red pepper flakes. Whisk well. Cut the pork into ¾-inch (2-cm) cubes, add to the marinade, and toss to coat all the pieces evenly. Cover and refrigerate for at least 12 hours or up to 18 hours.

Break up the bread into chunks and place in a small bowl. Add the vinegar, toss to coat, and allow to soften for about 10 minutes.

In a food processor, grind the almonds until grainy. Add the softened bread, tomatoes, remaining garlic, remaining 1 teaspoon paprika, the cayenne, and ¼ teaspoon salt and process until smooth. With the motor running, add the remaining olive oil in a slow, steady stream and process just until emulsified, or thoroughly blended. Taste and adjust the seasoning. Cover and refrigerate the sauce for 1 hour.

Prepare a fire in a grill, or preheat the broiler (grill). Remove the pork from the marinade and thread 2 or 3 cubes onto each skewer, pushing the cubes snugly together. If using wooden skewers, wrap about 2 inches (5 cm) of the blunt end of each skewer with aluminum foil to provide a handle and prevent burning. Pat the pork dry with paper towels. Place the skewers on the grill rack, handles facing outward, about 6 inches (15 cm) from the fire, or arrange on a broiler pan about 4 inches (10 cm) from the heat source. Grill or broil, turning once, until browned and firm, about 1½ minutes on each side.

Remove the foil from the skewers. Squeeze the lemon half over the skewers and serve at once with the sauce.

MAKES ABOUT 22 WARM BITES

TOASTING ALMONDS

To toast slivered almonds, spread a small amount in a dry frying pan on the stove top. Place over medium heat and toast, stirring frequently, until golden, about 5 minutes. Do not allow them to darken too much. Immediately transfer to a plate and let cool completely before using. Almonds continue to toast off the heat, so cook them a shade lighter than desired. Store toasted almonds in a closed container for 2–3 days at room temperature.

SMOKY SHRIMP
WITH GARLIC-PARSLEY MOJO

MESCAL

Mescal is a Mexican liquor distilled from the agave plant. All agave-based spirits, including tequila, are known collectively as mescals, but those bearing the name mescal are not necessarily made from the same variety of blue agave as tequilas. Mescal is generally a rustic drink with a bitter, pungent flavor. It suffuses this dish with a pleasant hint of smoke and cactus.

In a heavy frying pan over medium-low heat, warm the olive oil. Add the garlic and cook slowly, stirring frequently, until golden, about 3 minutes. Be careful not to let the garlic burn. Pour the garlic and oil into a shallow baking dish and let cool slightly. Add the mescal and the shrimp, toss to coat evenly, cover, and refrigerate for at least 3 hours or up to 6 hours, tossing occasionally.

Prepare a fire in an outdoor grill, or preheat a broiler (grill). To make the *mojo,* in a mini food processor, combine the olive oil, lime juice, garlic, cumin, parsley, and a rounded ½ teaspoon salt and pulse briefly to combine. (Or, place these ingredients in a bowl and whisk together vigorously.) Put the *mojo* in a small dish or ramekin and place in the center of a large platter.

Curl up 1 shrimp, tucking the thin tail end inside, and thread onto a skewer, piercing the shrimp in 3 places to hold it securely. Thread a second shrimp onto the skewer, keeping both shrimp close to the pointed end. Repeat with more skewers and the remaining shrimp. Wrap the blunt end of each skewer with aluminum foil halfway up its length to make a handle and to prevent the skewers from catching fire. Place the skewers on a grill rack about 6 inches (15 cm) above the fire, or arrange on a broiler pan and place under the broiler about 4 inches (10 cm) from the heat source. Grill or broil, turning once, until nicely charred and just opaque throughout, 2–3 minutes on each side.

Transfer the skewers to the platter, arranging them around the bowl of *mojo.* Serve at once.

Note: Mojo is a classic Cuban sauce that can feature any combination of citrus juice, fresh herbs, and garlic in a base of olive oil.

MAKES ABOUT 18 WARM BITES

¼ cup (2 fl oz / 60 ml) olive oil

4 large cloves garlic, thinly sliced

1 tablespoon best-quality mescal *(far left)*

2 lb (1 kg) large shrimp (prawns), peeled, deveined if desired (page 22)

FOR THE MOJO:

⅓ cup (3 fl oz / 80 ml) olive oil

⅓ cup (3 fl oz / 80 ml) fresh lime juice

1 tablespoon minced garlic (about 3 large cloves)

½ teaspoon ground cumin

⅓ cup (½ oz / 15 g) firmly packed finely chopped fresh flat-leaf (Italian) parsley

Salt

Wooden cocktail skewers soaked in water for 20–30 minutes

HORS D'OEUVRE BASICS

There are numerous occasions at which a selection of small hors d'oeuvres may be served. They might be a first course for a casual lunch with friends or passed on silver trays at a cocktail party. When deciding on a menu, consider the mood you wish to set. The recipes in this book are grouped into more casual hors d'oeuvres, for brunches or balmy afternoons, and more elegant ones for evening affairs. For a formal affair, the following section will help you plan out all the details.

STRIKING A BALANCE

When planning a formal party, one of the first questions is whether your selections will be treated as "buffet" or "passed" items. Buffet items are placed out in generous quantities for the guests to help themselves to as much as they would like. Passed items, on the other hand, might be offered to guests individually by the host, a willing guest, or a hired assistant. When items are passed, each guest might receive only one or two of each. Depending on the occasion, you may wish to create a more casual buffet atmosphere, a more elegant ambience where all offerings are passed, or a combination of the two.

The next considerations in choosing a menu are temperature, color, texture, and taste. The choices should be balanced among cold, warm, and room temperature, and should include something bright and vibrantly colored like Smoked Salmon Roulades (page 52) or Thai Guacamole (page 83) to attract the eye. Appeal to different tastes by including a spicy selection like Provençal Toasts (page 60) or Moroccan-Style Meatballs (page 17) along with a milder-flavored choice such as Goat Cheese Crisps with Mushroom Ragout (page 71).

Another question is what drinks will be served. Different hors d'oeuvres might seem right with wine, with Champagne, with a cocktail, or with fruit punch.

These are all considerations, but there are no hard-and-fast rules. Menu combinations are ultimately a matter of your personal taste and that of your guests.

ESTIMATING QUANTITY

Estimating the amount of food necessary for a get-together is a matter of preference, time, the nature of the party, and experience with certain groups of people. For instance, older people will generally eat less than younger people, men will generally eat more than women. Certain items that are perceived as delicacies, such as prawns or salmon, will disappear immediately. There are, however, some rules of thumb to estimate how much food to prepare.

Most guests will consume 8–10 "bites" total for every 60–90 minutes of a party. However, the larger the variety of offerings, the more hors d'oeuvres that will be consumed because everyone will want to try at least one of each item. At the beginning of a party, especially if it is in the early evening, the pace of eating will be more rapid, and it will slow as people satisfy their initial appetite.

If your party lasts longer than 90 minutes and is intended to replace dinner, the pace of eating will speed up again after the 2-hour mark. In this case, it is important to have enough hors d'oeuvres ready and waiting in the kitchen to replenish empty platters.

When the party is an average size, with 8–20 guests, count on 2 hot and

2 cold passed items, and 1 or 2 buffet items—5 or 6 selections in all. If there will be 30–40 guests, add 1 more of each hot and cold item, and 1 more buffet selection.

PLANNING AHEAD

In many recipes in this book, recipe steps that can be done in advance have been specified. Ideally, everything except the last-minute heating, cooking, and garnishing should be finished 30 minutes before your guests arrive, leaving you a little quiet time before the doorbell chimes. For a formal party, the host should not be cooking after the guests have arrived. If you will not have any help, choose items that can be assembled up to 30 minutes before serving, like New Potatoes with Caviar and Crème Fraîche (page 10), Vine Leaves Stuffed with Wild Rice and Apricots (page 98), Olives with Orange and Marjoram (page 32), Endive Boats with Smoked Salmon (page 18), Leek and Red Pepper Mini Quiches (page 14), or any of the dips and spreads. For a more casual party, friends could gather in the kitchen, making it possible to serve some of the last-minute items like Radicchio and Manchego Quesadillas (page 39), Oysters with a Garlic-Tarragon Crust (page 48), and Tempura Vegetables (page 94). Of course, always keep food safety in mind when considering which items can be made in advance (especially when serving raw meat or fish such as steak or tuna tartare). If you have any doubts about managing last-minute preparation, limit such items to smaller parties where there will be plenty of room in the fridge.

Assigning specific chores to helpers in advance is preferable to micromanaging the party while it is in full swing. Depending on the number of guests and the menu, helpers may be children or other family members, willing guests, hired help, or a combination of all. Try to anticipate every eventuality and plan for it with your helper(s) as far in advance as practicable. If you are darting around nervously, your guests are very unlikely to be able to relax.

PRESENTATION

Assemble a collection of flat round or oval platters, or use shiny metal-colored disposable platters. Whenever possible, line the edge of the platter with decorative greens such as ornamental kale, herb branches, edible flowers, or a combination of all three.

The most unattractive thing at a cocktail party is a messy, smeared platter with only one or two items left on it. Guests will be hesitant to take the last hors d'oeuvre from a platter. Be sure to replenish the platter as needed, wiping up any messy edges. If only a few hors d'oeuvres are left on a platter with no more in the kitchen, transfer the remaining items to a smaller dish.

Cocktail napkins, paper or fabric, should be readily available to your guests, especially when serving more messy items such as Polenta Crostini with Sausage Topping (page 72) or Crisp Oyster Skewers with Lemon Butter (page 90). Create decorative circles of napkins on the buffet surface and/or make sure anyone who passes a platter has a handful, fanned so that guests have no trouble taking just one napkin at a time.

Assign one helper to bus the party area regularly—an empty wineglass or a wadded-up napkin should not remain in evidence for long. Ashtrays should be placed in plain sight and emptied as often as possible.

Make sure that there are enough glasses and small plates, if you are using them, to resupply each guest at least twice without having to wash them. Renting equipment for a party can be expensive, but it may be the best option if you're having a sizable party and would like to have everything match.

LIBATIONS

Depending on your event, you may wish to serve an assortment of alcoholic beverages, including cocktails. Among the following recipes is a drink to pair with every appetizer.

MIDTOWN MANHATTAN

Ice cubes

3 fl oz (90 ml) premium or super-premium bourbon whiskey

1 fl oz (30 ml) sweet vermouth

1 drop Angostura bitters

Dash of Bénédictine

1 maraschino cherry

Chill a stemmed cocktail glass. Half-fill a cocktail shaker with ice and add the bourbon, vermouth, bitters, and Bénédictine. Cover and shake vigorously about 40 times. Strain into the chilled glass and garnish with the cherry. Serve at once. Makes 1 cocktail.

THE CHURCHILL MARTINI

3 fl oz (90 ml) Plymouth gin

8 ice cubes

Twist of lemon zest

Chill a martini glass. Combine the gin and ice in a cocktail shaker or pitcher and shake or stir 50 times. Strain the cocktail into the chilled glass. Immediately bruise the lemon zest directly over the surface of the liquid, drop it in, and serve. Makes 1 cocktail.

SAKE MARTINI

1 pt (16 fl oz/500 ml) Japanese vodka such as Suntory or any premium vodka

1 piece English (hothouse) cucumber, 4 inches (10 cm) long, peeled and halved lengthwise, plus 4–6 peeled thin slices

Ice cubes

4 fl oz (125 ml) good-quality dry sake

In a clean glass jar, combine the vodka and the cucumber halves. Seal well and let stand at room temperature for 6 days.

Chill 4–6 martini glasses in the freezer for at least 30 minutes. Remove the cucumber halves from the vodka and discard them. Half-fill a large cocktail pitcher with ice, add the vodka and sake, and stir about 50 times. Strain into the chilled glasses and garnish each drink with a cucumber slice. Serve immediately. Makes 4–6 cocktails.

FRENCH 75

Ice cubes, plus 4 extra for serving

4 fl oz (125 ml) Cognac or Armagnac

2 fl oz (60 ml) fresh lemon juice

2 teaspoons sugar

6–8 fl oz (180–250 ml) chilled Champagne

Chill 2 Champagne flutes. Half-fill a cocktail shaker with ice cubes and add the Cognac, lemon juice, and sugar. Cover and shake vigorously. Strain into the chilled flutes. Add 2 ice cubes to each flute and top off with the Champagne. Stir gently and serve at once. Makes 2 cocktails.

CUBAN MOJITO

8 fresh mint leaves

1 tablespoon Simple Syrup (recipe follows)

1 tablespoon fresh lime juice

Crushed ice

2 fl oz (60 ml) white rum

Club soda, as needed

½ fl oz (15 ml) dark rum

In a tall tumbler, combine the mint, syrup, and lime juice. "Muddle" or pound lightly with a muddler or the handle end of a wooden spoon to release the flavor of the mint. Fill the glass with crushed ice and add the white rum. Fill the glass almost to the top with club soda and carefully "float" the dark rum on the top. Serve at once. Makes 1 cocktail.

SIMPLE SYRUP

Simple syrup is a bartender's best friend, as it makes sweetening cocktails easy—coaxing granulated sugar to dissolve in cold liquid is no small feat. Combine ½ cup (4 oz/125 g) sugar and ½ cup (4 fl oz/125 ml) water in a small saucepan and stir over low heat until the sugar dissolves. Remove from the heat, let cool, and place in a clean squeeze bottle or glass jar. Refrigerate and use as needed. It will keep almost indefinitely.

BRAZILIAN BOMBSHELL

Ice cubes

1½ teaspoons fresh lemon juice

¾ fl oz (20 ml) Rose's Lime Juice

¼ cup (2 fl oz/60 ml) pineapple juice

¾ fl oz (20 ml) cachaça (Brazilian sugarcane brandy)

1½ fl oz (45 ml) silver tequila

Chill a stemmed cocktail glass. Half-fill a cocktail shaker with ice and add the lemon juice, lime juice, pineapple juice, cachaça, and tequila. Cover and shake vigorously about 40 times. Strain into the chilled glass and serve at once. Makes 1 cocktail.

OYSTER SHOOTERS

1 ripe avocado

6 fl oz (180 ml) premium vodka, chilled

¼ teaspoon pure chile powder

12 small oysters, shucked (see page 48), or 3 preshucked Western oysters, quartered

1½ teaspoons minced fresh cilantro (fresh coriander)

Chill 12 shot glasses, preferably straight sided. Just before serving, pit and peel the avocado, then cut into small dice. Working quickly, place 1 tablespoon vodka into each of the chilled glasses and sprinkle with just a few grains of the chile powder. Top each with an oyster, a few cubes of avocado, and ⅛ teaspoon cilantro. Serve immediately, instructing your guests to drink the whole thing in a single gulp. Makes 12 cocktails.

WHITE WINE SANGRIA

1 bottle (750 ml) Spanish dry white wine such as Albariño or white Rioja

1 lemon, peeled in a continuous thin spiral and flesh thinly sliced crosswise

1 orange, peeled in a continuous thin spiral and flesh thinly sliced crosswise

1 fl oz (30 ml) brandy, or to taste

1 fl oz (30 ml) Triple Sec, Cointreau, or Curaçao, or to taste

1 tablespoon superfine (caster) sugar or Simple Syrup (page 108), or to taste

1 ripe peach, pitted and sliced

½ cup (2 oz/60 g) sliced strawberries or other soft fruits in season (optional)

½ cup (3 oz/90 g) seedless green grapes, halved (optional)

1 cup (8 fl oz/250 ml) chilled club soda

Ice cubes

In a large pitcher, combine the wine, lemon and orange peels and sliced fruit, brandy, Triple Sec, and sugar. Stir to dissolve the sugar and taste. Adjust with sugar, brandy, or Triple Sec to the desired flavor, remembering that it will be diluted further with the soda and ice. Cover the pitcher and refrigerate for 2–3 hours. Remove from the refrigerator and add the peach and, if using, the strawberries and grapes. Re-cover and return to the refrigerator for 2 hours but no longer.

Just before serving, add the soda and ice cubes and stir. Or, place the ice cubes in tumblers. Pour out the sangria, ladle the fruits into the glasses, and serve. Makes 1 pitcher.

BLOOD ORANGE DAIQUIRI

¼ cup (2 fl oz/60 ml) fresh blood orange juice

1½ teaspoons fresh lime juice

1 teaspoon Simple Syrup (page 108)

2 fl oz (60 ml) white rum

½ fl oz (15 ml) dark rum

Chill a stemmed cocktail glass. Combine the orange juice, lime juice, syrup, and both rums in a cocktail shaker. Cover and shake vigorously about 50 times. Strain into the chilled glass and serve. Makes 1 cocktail.

FRESH WATERMELON MARGARITA

¼–½ watermelon

Ice cubes

4 fl oz (125 ml) premium silver tequila

2 fl oz (60 ml) Triple Sec or Cointreau

3 tablespoons fresh orange juice

2 tablespoons fresh lime juice

2–3 teaspoons Simple Syrup (page 108)

4 paper-thin lime slices

Cut the watermelon into chunks, scrape out the seeds, and purée in a blender. Half-fill a pitcher with ice and add 1 cup (8 fl oz/250 ml) watermelon purée, tequila, Triple Sec, orange juice, lime juice, and syrup to taste. Stir briskly about 40 times. Half-fill 4 large wine-glasses with ice and pour the mixture over the ice. Cut halfway through each lime slice, perch a slice on the edge of each glass, and serve. Makes 4 cocktails.

GLOSSARY

ASIAN FISH SAUCE Southeast Asians use fish sauce in the same way that Westerners use salt, both as a cooking seasoning and at the table. Made from salted and fermented fish, it is a thin, clear liquid that ranges in color from amber to dark brown. Famous for its pungent aroma and strong, salty flavor, it is often mixed with other ingredients and used as a dipping sauce. Fish sauce is called *nam pla* in Thailand, *nuoc mam* in Vietnam, *tuk trey* in Cambodia, and *patis* in the Philippines.

AVOCADO Rich in flavor and silky in texture, avocados are a favorite subtropical fruit. To prepare an avocado for dicing, use a small, sharp knife to carefully cut it in half lengthwise around the large, round pit at the center. Rotate the halves in opposite directions to separate them and remove the pit with the tip of a spoon and discard. Peel away the skin with the knife or ease a large spoon between the avocado flesh and the peel and gently scoop out the flesh, scraping as close to the peel as possible.

BALSAMIC VINEGAR A specialty of the Italian region of Emilia-Romagna, primarily the town of Modena, balsamic vinegar is an aged vinegar made from the unfermented grape juice, or must, of white Trebbiano grapes. Aged in a series of wooden casks of decreasing sizes, each of a different wood, balsamic grows sweeter and more mellow with time. Long-aged balsamic vinegar is syrupy, intense, and intended to be used in small quantities as a condiment.

BEEF, RAW Eating raw beef always entails some degree of risk of bacterial contamination, including *E. coli*. The latter can make a healthy adult ill; the risk is greater for the very young, the elderly, pregnant women, or those with compromised immune systems.

BELL PEPPER Also called sweet peppers or capsicums, bell peppers may be green, red, yellow, orange, brown, or purple. To core and seed a bell pepper, cut the pepper in half crosswise or lengthwise and remove the stem along with the cluster of seeds with your hands or a knife. Trim away the remaining seeds and white membranes, or ribs, and cut to desired size and shape.

BLUE CHEESES Although they were developed at roughly the same time, Italy's Gorgonzola is very different from Roquefort, France's premiere blue cheese. Roquefort is made from sheep's milk and is crumbly and quite salty, while Gorgonzola, made from cow's milk, is creamy, sweet, and earthy. Stilton, a British blue cheese, is well aged and has a firm yet crumbly texture. In its finer versions, it is quite strong and almost orange in color.

BREAD CRUMBS, DRIED To make dried bread crumbs, dry out the bread in a 200°F (95°C) oven for about 1 hour. Break the bread into bite-sized pieces and process in a blender or food processor into fine crumbs. Dried bread crumbs will keep for up to 1 month in the refrigerator. For fresh bread crumbs, see page 90.

BUTTER An essential dairy product, butter is made by churning or agitating cream until the fats separate from the liquids and produce a semisolid form. Butter is sold in two basic styles. More familiar is salted butter, although many cooks prefer unsalted butter. Unsalted butter, also called sweet butter, is favored because it lacks the additional salt that can interfere with the taste of the final recipe. It also is likely to be fresher since salt often acts as a preservative, prolonging butter's shelf life.

CHERVIL A springtime herb with curly, dark green leaves, chervil is best when used fresh in salads, with vegetables, or with eggs. It has mild flavor reminiscent of parsley and anise.

CHILES, HANDLING To reduce the heat of a chile, cut out the membranes, or ribs, and discard the seeds. This is where the capsaicin, the hot element of a chile, is concentrated. If you like heat, leave in a few seeds. Avoid touching your eyes, mouth, or other sensitive areas while you are working with chiles. When finished, thoroughly wash your hands, the cutting board, and the knife with hot, soapy water. Consider wearing kitchen gloves when working with especially hot chiles to prevent burns to your fingers.

Following are some common chile types used in the recipes in this book:

Scotch Bonnet: Only 1 to 1½ inches (2.5 to 4 cm) long, the Scotch bonnet is extremely hot. These round fresh chiles are green, yellow, orange, or red.

Serrano: This chile is similar to the familiar jalapeño in heat intensity, but the serrano is sleeker and has a distinctly sharp taste. About 2 inches (5 cm) long, serranos may be green or red. Most often, they are used fresh.

Thai: Also known as a bird chile, this very hot, thin green or red chile is usually only about 1 inch (2.5 cm) long.

CHILE PASTE A popular Asian seasoning, chile paste is made with chopped or ground hot chiles, salt, and usually vinegar. Depending on the place of origin, different seasonings, such as garlic, ginger, soybeans, sesame oil, and even sugar, are added. Just a touch of the paste adds a rich, fiery taste.

CRÈME FRAÎCHE A soured cultured cream product, originally from France, crème fraîche is similar to sour cream but sweeter and more indulgent. Crème fraîche is not always easy to find, but home cooks can make their own. To make crème fraîche, combine 1 cup (8 fl oz/250 ml) heavy (double) cream and 1 tablespoon buttermilk in a small saucepan over medium-low heat. Heat to lukewarm, and do not allow to simmer. Remove from the heat, cover, and allow to thicken at warm room temperature, which can take from 8 to 48 hours. Once it is as thick and flavorful as you want it, chill it before using.

CUCUMBER Slicing cucumbers are the smooth, slender, dark green vegetables that regularly show up in green salads, on crudité platters, and as a garnish on cold plates. They are available in two varieties: outdoor and English, or hothouse. Outdoor varieties should be 8–10 inches (20–25 cm) long and 1–1½ inches (2.5–4 cm) in diameter, and they are often coated with wax. Avoid waxed cucumbers if possible, as waxed skin must be peeled, and with the skin goes the vitamin A. English cucumbers should be 12–16 inches (30–40 cm) long and have thin, smooth skin. They are virtually seedless.

To seed a cucumber, cut the cucumber in half lengthwise. Use a melon baller or spoon to scoop out the seeds and the surrounding pulpy matter.

DUCK The most commonly marketed duck breeds are White Pekin (also known as Long Island), Muscovy, and Moulard, the last a cross between the first two. The breasts of Moulard are generally leaner than the other two because much of their fat is concentrated in their livers, which are sold as foie gras.

EGG, RAW Eggs are sometimes used raw in dressings and other preparations. Raw eggs run a risk of being infected with salmonella or other bacteria, which can lead to food poisoning. This risk is of most concern to small children, older people, pregnant women, and anyone with a compromised immune system. If you have health and safety concerns, do not consume raw egg, or seek out a pasteurized egg product to replace it. Eggs can also be made safe by heating them to a temperature of 160°F (71°C). Note that coddled, poached, and soft-boiled eggs do not reach this temperature.

EGG WHITES, BEATING When beating egg whites, start with a spotlessly clean bowl, preferably stainless steel or copper, and a whisk. Hand-beating egg whites with a whisk incorporates the most air, yielding a very stable foam. Food processors and blenders do not aerate the whites as well. Beat egg whites thoroughly. Once the whites foam, they will begin to increase in volume and will become opaque. Lift the whisk from the whites to determine the state of their peaks. When the whites are beaten to soft peaks, the peaks will gently fall over to one side, while whites beaten to stiff, dry peaks will stand upright. Do not overbeat egg whites, or they will become clumpy and grainy.

EMULSION An emulsion is a stable mixture that contains two or more liquids that would ordinarily not combine, such as oil and vinegar. An emulsion requires vigorous shaking or whisking as well as an agent known as an emulsifier to help hold the other ingredients together. Common emulsifiers include egg yolks, mustard, and cream.

FOLDING A method used to combine two ingredients or mixtures with different densities, folding is a simple but crucial technique. Light, airy mixtures such as egg whites or whipped cream will lose their loft if incorrectly stirred into heavier batters. To fold, spoon one-fourth of the lighter mixture atop the heavier mixture. With a long-handled rubber spatula, slice down through both mixtures and sweep the spatula along the bottom of the bowl. Bring the spatula with a gentle circular motion up and over the contents. The goal is to lift up some of the heavier batter from the bottom of the bowl and gently "fold" it over the top of the lighter mixture without deflating the lighter mixture. Rotate the pan or bowl a quarter turn and repeat the down-across-up-over motion, gradually adding the rest of the lighter mixture to the heavier. Continue in this manner,

rotating the bowl with each fold, just until the lighter mixture is incorporated. Use a firm but light hand and don't overmix.

FROMAGE BLANC Literally "white cheese," this French term refers to a wide variety of unripened creamy cheeses made from skim or whole milk, with or without cream added. Fromage blanc is commonly eaten flavored with sugar as a simple dessert and is also used in cooking.

HERBS, MINCING Many recipes in this book and elsewhere call for minced fresh herbs. Begin with dry herbs; wet ones will stick to the knife. Remove the leaves and discard the stems. Then, keeping the fingers safely clear, chop the leaves with a good-sized chef's knife, holding down the knife tip with one hand so that it never leaves the cutting board and moving your chopping wrist and hand rhythmically. Gather the herb repeatedly into smaller and tighter clumps and chop until it is as fine as you want it. Using a pair of kitchen scissors to snip herbs may be even easier than mincing in some cases, especially for chives.

HOISIN SAUCE A thick, sweet, reddish brown Chinese sauce made from soy-beans, sugar, garlic, five-spice powder or star anise, and a hint of chile. It can be thick and creamy or thin enough to pour. It is rubbed on meat and poultry

before roasting to give them a sweet flavor and red color and sometimes appears as a condiment. Hoisin sauce should be used judiciously, as its strong flavor can easily overpower most foods.

JULIENNING A technique by which food is cut into thin matchstick strips. Vegetables are the most common candidates for julienning, but meat and cheese may be prepared in this way, too. To julienne, cut the food into pieces the length of the desired julienne strips. Cut each piece lengthwise into slices as thick as the desired julienne. Stack the slices and cut them lengthwise into strips.

LEMON Lemon is an important seasoning in the kitchen, and its juice can add a fruity zing to almost any dish. To juice a lemon, store it at room temperature and roll it firmly against a hard, flat surface or between your palms to crush some of its inner membrane. Slice the lemon in half crosswise and use a reamer with fluted edges to extract every last drop of juice. Take care not to rub too hard, though, or you will crush the pith and infuse the juice with some of its bitterness. A fork inserted into the cut surface of the lemon then rotated back and forth will work almost as well as a reamer.

MADEIRA A fortified wine origin-ating on, or made in the style of, the Portuguese island of Madeira. Stored for at least 3 months in a warm room or tank, and then sometimes further aged in wooden casks, the wine gradually develops a distinctive flavor reminiscent of burnt caramel. Madeiras vary from mellow and nutty-tasting dry types to sweet, robust after-dinner beverages.

MASCARPONE Thick enough to spread when chilled, but sufficiently fluid to pour at room temperature, this Italian cream cheese is noted for its rich flavor and acidic tang. Similar to crème fraîche, it is sold in tubs in well-stocked food stores and in the cheese cases of Italian delicatessens.

MELON BALLER Also known as a vegetable scoop, potato baller, or melon-ball scoop, this hand tool has a small bowl at one end, about 1 inch (2.5 cm) in diameter, used for making decorative balls from melon or other semifirm foods. It is useful for seeding or coring some foods, such as cucumbers, or preparing them for stuffing. Some scoops have a second, slightly smaller bowl at the opposite end of the handle.

MINI FOOD PROCESSOR Called for in many of the recipes in this book, the mini food processor is a real convenience to the cook. It simplifies making small amounts of bread crumbs, mincing fresh herbs, or creating a few spoonfuls of a flavored butter. When working with smaller quantities, any recipe step that is usually executed in a larger processor will be more efficient in the mini unit, as there will be less waste.

MINI MUFFIN PAN A pan specially designed for baking miniature muffins, with cups each 1¾ inches (4.5 cm) in diameter. Seek out a nonstick version.

MIRIN Extracted from fermented sweet rice and usually referred to as sweet rice wine, amber-colored mirin is a popular seasoning in Japanese kitchens. Store bottles of mirin away from heat and light to safeguard their flavor and color.

MUSTARD, JAPANESE This dry mustard sold in Japanese markets is quite strong. To prepare it, add enough water to make a stiff paste and then let it stand for 10 minutes. Mix only as much as you plan to use immediately, as the flavor will dissipate with time. Japanese mustard is also available in tubes, which must be kept refrigerated. A strong, hot dry mustard may be substituted, or even a prepared mustard, as long as it is not too vinegary or sweet.

NONALUMINUM Selecting a cookware made from a nonreactive material such as stainless steel, enamel, or glass is important when cooking with acidic ingredients such as citrus juice, vinegar, wine, tomatoes, and most vegetables. Cookware made with materials such as aluminum (and, to a lesser degree, cast iron or unlined copper) will react with acidic ingredients and will impart a metallic taste and grayish color.

PARMESAN CHEESE Parmesan cheese is a firm, aged, salty cheese made from

cow's milk. True Parmesan comes from the Emilia-Romagna region of northern Italy and is referred to by its trade-marked name, Parmigiano-Reggiano. Rich and complex in flavor and often possessing a pleasant granular texture, this savory cheese is best when grated only as needed just before use in a recipe or at the table.

PEPPER, WHITE Made from peppercorns that have had their skins removed and berries dried, white pepper is often less aromatic and more mild in flavor than black pepper. It is favored in the preparation of light-colored sauces and dips when cooks want to avoid flecks of black pepper in the final dish.

PERNOD This liqueur is an absinthe substitute made by Pernod et Fils in France, a company that produced true absinthe before it was banned in 1914. Although far sweeter than absinthe, Pernod shares its anise flavor. Pernod is yellowish and turns cloudy when mixed with water. Pastis, a similar product also made by the Pernod firm and others, is based on licorice instead of anise.

POTATOES, NEW Harvested in spring and early summer, new potatoes are usually quite small and of the round red or round white varieties. They are low in starch and will keep their shape well after cooking. Be aware that not all small red and white potatoes are new. A true new potato is freshly harvested, will have a thin skin, and will not keep long.

QUARK This fresh curd cheese is German in origin and is made of skimmed milk. It is a neutral-tasting soft cheese that is milder in flavor but richer in texture than low-fat yogurt. Quark comes in nonfat and richer low-fat varieties and is often used in dips, salads, and sauces.

RADICCHIO A variety of chicory native to Italy and characterized by its variegated purplish red leaves and bitter taste. The sturdy raw leaves hold up well, and their assertive flavor is nicely matched with cheeses, cured meats, anchovies, olives, and capers. Crisp and brightly colored, radicchio grows in round or elongated heads. It complements many ingredients with its deep ruby red color and pleasantly bitter flavor.

RENDERING A process in which animal fat is melted over low heat to separate the pure fat from bits of meaty tissue. As the fat melts, it separates from the bits of meat called cracklings, which sink to the bottom of the pan. The pure, clear fat is then strained to remove these darker bits.

SESAME OIL, ASIAN Sold in small bottles in Asian markets and well-stocked food stores, this oil is pressed from toasted sesame seeds, resulting in a dark amber color and a full, rich, nutty flavor. It is used almost always as a seasoning. Do not substitute sesame oil made from untoasted seeds.

SHALLOT A small member of the onion family that looks like a large clove of garlic covered with papery bronze or reddish skin. Shallots have white flesh streaked with purple, a crisp texture, and a flavor more subtle than that of an onion. They are often used for flavoring recipes that would be overpowered by the stronger taste of onion.

SUGAR, SUPERFINE When finely ground, granulated sugar becomes superfine sugar, also known as castor or caster sugar. Because it dissolves rapidly, it is preferred for cold recipes such as mixed drinks (it is also sold as bar sugar) and for delicate mixtures such as beaten egg whites.

TAPENADE A classic Provençal olive spread made from capers, anchovies, and garlic. The ingredients are mashed into a paste, preferably in a mortar with a pestle, and the paste is used as a spread for grilled bread, smeared on pizzas, or used as a dip for vegetables and crudités. Both green and black tapenades, made from either green or black olives, are available. See also page 36.

TOMATOES, CANNED Canned plum (Roma) tomatoes from southern Italy are famous for their high quality, and they are well worth seeking out when buying canned tomatoes. Other canned tomatoes can be acceptable as well, especially whole peeled tomatoes packed in enamel-lined cans, which cut down on the metallic taste many canned foods pick up. Whatever variety you choose, buy whole peeled tomatoes, not the crushed variety, which are sometimes packed with tomato paste or purée.

TUNA, AHI A prized food fish, tuna comes from a family of large fish with rich, oily, firm flesh. Yellowfin tuna, which can weigh up to 300 pounds (150 kg), is also known as ahi, the Hawaiian term for the fish. It has slightly more flavor than albacore and is typically cooked until seared on the outside and rare on the inside. Fresh ahi is also used for sashimi and sushi.

ZESTER A handheld tool with a row of circular holes at the end of its metal blade, specially designed to remove zest from citrus efficiently. For more information, see page 87.

INDEX

SIMON & SCHUSTER SOURCE
A Division of Simon & Schuster
Rockefeller Center, 1230 Avenue of the Americas,
New York, NY 10020

WILLIAMS-SONOMA
Founder and Vice-Chairman: Chuck Williams
Book Buyer: Cecilia Michaelis

WELDON OWEN INC.
Chief Executive Officer: John Owen
President: Terry Newell
Chief Operating Officer: Larry Partington
Vice President, International Sales: Stuart Laurence
Creative Director: Gaye Allen
Series Editor: Sarah Putman Clegg
Associate Editor: Heather Belt
Copy Editor: Sharon Silva
Consulting Editor: Norman Kolpas
Designers: Lisa Schulz, Douglas Chalk
Production Manager: Chris Hemesath
Production Assistant: Donita Boles
Studio Manager: Brynn Breuner
Production Designer: Joan Olson
Photograph Editor: Lisa Lee
Food Photographer: Noel Barnhurst
Food Stylist: Sandra Cook
Indexer: Ken DellaPenta
Proofreaders: Desne Border, Ken DellaPenta,
Kate Chynoweth, Carrie Bradley, Arin Hailey

Williams-Sonoma Collection *Hors d'Oeuvre* was
conceived and produced by Weldon Owen Inc.,
814 Montgomery Street, San Francisco,
California 94133, in collaboration with
Williams-Sonoma, 3250 Van Ness Avenue,
San Francisco, California 94109.

A Weldon Owen Production
Copyright © 2001 by Weldon Owen Inc. and
Williams-Sonoma Inc.

SIMON & SCHUSTER SOURCE and colophon are
registered trademarks of Simon & Schuster, Inc.

Set in Trajan, Utopia, and Vectora.

Color separations by Bright Arts Graphics
Singapore (Pte.) Ltd.
Printed and bound in Singapore by Tien Wah
Press (Pte.) Ltd.

First printed in 2001.

10 9 8 7 6 5 4

Library of Congress Cataloging-in-Publication
Data is available.

ISBN 0-7432-2442-6

A NOTE ON WEIGHTS AND MEASURES

All recipes include customary U.S. and metric measurements. Metric conversions are based on
a standard developed for these books and have been rounded off. Actual weights may vary.